Super BIBLE ACTIVITIES

FOR KIDS

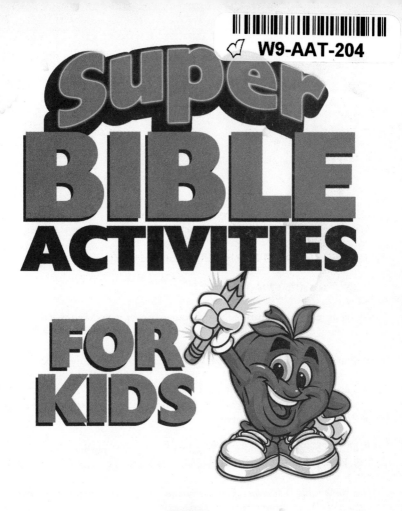

BARBOUR
PUBLISHING

Bible Activities © 1998 by Barbour Publishing, Inc.
More Bible Activities © 1999 by Barbour Publishing, Inc.

Super Bible Activities © 2009 by Barbour Publishing, Inc.

ISBN 978-1-60260-394-3

Scripture quotations are taken from the King James Version of the Bible.

Scripture quotations are taken from the HOLY BIBLE: NEW INTERNATIONAL VERSION ® 1973, 1978, 1984 by International Bible Society. Used by permission of Zondervan. All rights reserved.

Published by Barbour Books, an imprint of Barbour Publishing, Inc., P.O. Box 719, Uhrichsville, Ohio 44683, www.barbourbooks.com

Our mission is to publish and distribute inspirational products offering exceptional value and biblical encouragement to the masses.

Member of the
Evangelical Christian
Publishers Association

Printed in the United States of America.

WORD SCRAMBLES
THINGS IN THE TABERNACLE

1. TICUSNRA _____

2. AMLADNPTS _____

3. RAALT _____

4. SNECIEN _____

5. LIVE _____

6. ETGA _____

7. BTEAL _____

8. KAR _____

9. LOI _____

10. VRLAE _____

BIBLE CROSS OUTS

Cross off the letters that occur four times. The letters
that are left will spell out the answers.

J	D	Q	K	A	C	M	V
R	B	I	U	■	D	W	Q
G	W	M	O	C	R	L	F
F	I	R	W	A	J	B	T
Q	B	■	K	M	H	U	J
P	M	C	H	J	F	I	U
K	L	I	U	S	R	W	T
I	B	F	N	Q	E	K	C

1. What future king of Israel killed a giant as a youth?

2. What was the giant's name?

3. What nationality was the giant?

4

WORD MATCH

Match the words with their definitions by drawing
lines to connect them.

1. IMAGE	1. DIRTY
2. KID	2. THE HIGHEST POINT
3. STATUTES	3. DANGER
4. PINNACLE	4. JERUSALEM
5. LOOKINGGLASSES	5. LAWS
6. JEOPARDY	6. BABY GOAT
7. HUSBANDMAN	7. LETTERS
8. EPISTLES	8. MIRRORS
9. ZION	9. FARMER
10. UNWASHEN	10. IDOLS

CROSSWORD

ACROSS

1. Person who speaks Arabic
5. "Hearken unto me, my people; and give _____ unto me" (Isa. 51:4)
8. Infant
9. Pimple, slang
10. People who swing
12. All right
13. The king of the Amalekites that Samuel cut into pieces (1 Sam. 15:33)
16. Three, in Roman numerals
19. Things that drip
21. To be sick
22. Esau's father-in-law (Gen. 26:34)
23. Mountain, abbr.
24. "I beheld, and, lo, there _____ _____ no man, and all the birds of the heavens were fled" (2 words) (Jer. 4:25)

DOWN

1. Stomach muscles, for short
2. Not cooked
3. One of King David's wives (1 Sam. 25:39)
4. Benjamin, for short
5. Belonging to one of the prophets

6. What we breathe
7. Routes, abbr.
11. "_____ ye into all the world, and preach the gospel" (Mark 16:15)
13. The first man
14. What some people do to their teeth while they're sleeping
15. General practitioner, abbr.
17. Metal
18. "There _____ _____ God like thee in the heaven" (2 words) (2 Chron. 6:14)
20. A green vegetable

7

WORD SCRAMBLES
NEW TESTAMENT BOOKS #1

1. STAC _____

2. KLUE _____

3. ANESIPESH _____

4. NROSMA _____

5. IRACHIOTSNN _____

6. NJOH _____

7. NAAALGSIT _____

8. RKMA _____

9. THAEWTM _____

BIBLE CROSS OUTS

Cross off the letters that occur five times. The letters
that are left will spell out the answers.

A	G	C	T	J	F	H	B	Z
Z	O	K	P	U	M	K	S	J
B	C	A	J	P	N	P	D	Z
D	F	M	E	P	G	L	F	B
G	I	C	M	L	B	P	A	Z
F	K	H	T	Z	W	E	G	K
N	T	M	Y	G	M	C	Y	C
F	B	E	K	A	R	J	S	J

1. How many Philistines did Samson kill with the
   jawbone of a donkey?

2. Who betrayed him?

3. How long was Samson a judge of Israel?

9

WORD SEARCH
ANIMALS IN THE BIBLE

After you've found all the words in the word search, find all the unused letters in the puzzle. Unscramble them to find the hidden words.

WORD LIST

BEAR	LION
BITTERN	MOLE
CAMEL	MOUSE
DEER	OWL
DOG	PIG
EAGLE	RAM
FERRET	ROEBUCK
FOX	TORTOISE
GOAT	UNICORN
HART	WEASEL
HORSE	WOLF

```
R E E L G I P I R T
N T B S W R A M E F
R W E U I O M X E E
E E A S N O L O D R
T A R E R I T F L R
T S E S S O C R R E
I E L U N G H O O T
B L G O D O O A R T
C C A M E L I A R N
R O E B U C K L T T
```

11

WORD SCRAMBLES
PEOPLE & THINGS ON NOAH'S ARK

1. IEWSV   _____

2. EMLEAFS   _____

3. EMLAS   _____

4. HMSE   _____

5. OLWF   _____

6. MHA   _____

7. AHTEJHP   _____

8. EBSAST   _____

9. LECTTA   _____

10. OHAN   _____

TRUE or FALSE

		TRUE	FALSE
1.	Goliath had six fingers on each hand and six toes on each foot.	☐	☐
2.	The dove was the only bird Noah sent out to find dry land.	☐	☐
3.	Obed was Ruth's first baby.	☐	☐
4.	Jesus was baptized in the Jordan River.	☐	☐
5.	Jesus fed 6,000 people with 8 loaves and 4 fishes.	☐	☐
6.	Lazarus was in the grave 3 days when Jesus raised him from the dead.	☐	☐
7.	Moses parted the Dead Sea with his rod.	☐	☐
8.	John the Baptist died a normal death.	☐	☐
9.	The serpent tempted Eve with an apple.	☐	☐
10.	David killed Goliath with his own (Goliath's) sword.	☐	☐

BIBLE TRIVIA

The name of the first woman was:
- a) Evelyn
- b) Rachel
- c) Eve
- d) Rebekah

Did you know that
the first woman's name means
"mother of all living?"
(GENESIS 3:20)

WORD SCRAMBLES
OLD TESTAMENT BOOKS #1

1. DGSUJE   _____

2. UBRNMSE   _____

3. RUTYOEEODNM   _____

4. USXEDO   _____

5. GSINK   _____

6. IEGNSSE   _____

7. SUIEIVLTC   _____

8. UJOAHS   _____

9. UHRT   _____

10. LMSAUE   _____

CRYPT-CROSS

Now when they heard this, they were pricked in their heart, and said unto Peter and to the rest of the apostles, kli (12 across) and brethren, what gncff (13 across) we ma (10 across)? Then Peter said unto them, Vlslir (5 down), and be baptized every one of you qi (22 down) the ickl (6 across) of Jesus Christ for the vlkqggqai (18 across) of sins, and ul (23 down) shall vlblqyl (8 across) the gift of the Holy Ghost. For the promise qg (9 across) unto you, and ra (15 across) your children, and to all that cvl (17 down) afar aww (19 down), lyli (1 down) as many as the Lord our God shall call. And with many arnlv (16 down) words mqm (14 across) he rlgrqwu (21 across) and exhort, gcuqio (2 across), gcyl (2 down) uahvglfylg (3 down) from this untoward olilvcrqai (4 down). Then they that gladly received his word zlvl (20 across) tcsrqxlm (11 down): and the same day there were added unto them about three thousand souls. And they continued stedfastly in the csagrflg' (7 down) doctrine and fellowship, and in breaking of bread, and in prayers. (ACTS 2:37-42)

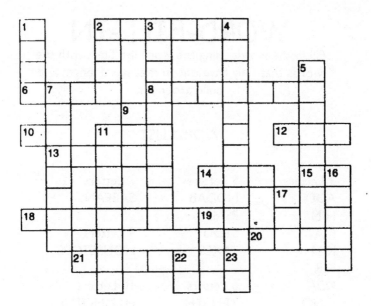

O C A K X L S U N Q M E D H G J I T P B Y R F Z V W
A B C D E F G H I J K L M N O P Q R S T U V W X Y Z

17

WORD-FILL-IN

Fill in the words using the word list. Start with the
words that only have one in that word length and
build around it.

WORD LIST

3 Letters
ADD
HIN
IRA
KIN
KIR
KOA
ONO
WIT

4 Letters
ENDS
IRAM
KORE

5 Letters
NODAB
PSALM
STOUT
TAXES

6 Letters
KENATH
KOHATH
TEMENI

7 Letters
SABEANS

9 Letters
HOUSETOPS

10 Letters
HAMMOTHDOR
WORSHIPPED

10-LETTER ACROSTIC

Solve the clues for each word across.
The circled letter is the first letter of the next word.

1. Person in charge of a group
2. Not really wanting to
3. Using mostly the left hand
4. People from different countries
5. Comes after seventeenth
6. Gossip
7. The _____ snowman
8. "Jeiel, _____, Zabad..." (Ezra 10:43)
9. A male slave
10. Pay back
11. "Affliction and our _____?" (Psalm 44:24)
12. Major tremor of the Earth
13. Carvings
14. People who live near you, Old English
15. To feel fresh again, Old English
16. Dependability
17. In agreement
18. Sewing, crocheting, knitting, etc.
19. "...and _____," (Ezek. 25:9)
20. "..._____. And Kohath..." (Num. 26:58)

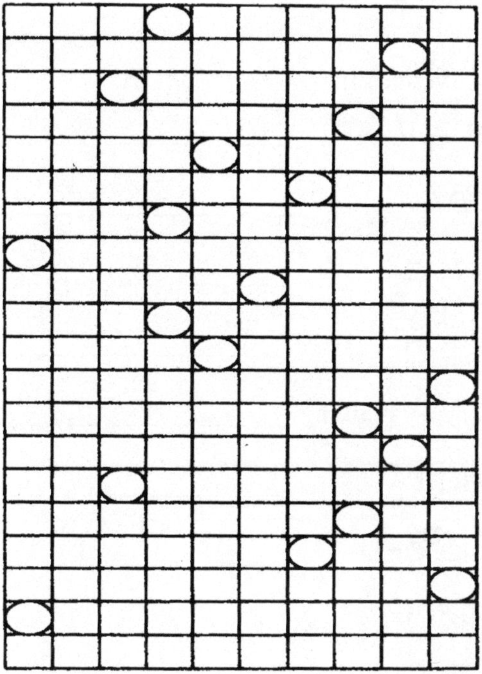

WORD SCRAMBLES
GOOD KINGS IN THE BIBLE

1. AHOJS _____

2. RAHZAIA _____

3. ADDVI _____

4. IAHMAZA _____

5. MJATOH _____

6. EOTJHAPHSAH _____

7. AJHOSI _____

8. ONOSOML _____

9. IHHKAZEE _____

10. AAS _____

11. ZIAZHU _____

BIBLE CROSS OUTS

Cross off the letters that occur five times. The letters
that are left will spell out the answers.

X	J	G	W	E	L	R	W	K
I	W	C	M	P	H	Z	O	Q
Q	R	X	A	F	L	H	K	A
G	W	K	Q	B	Y	S	Z	P
E	Y	V	P	Z	E	M	N	X
F	S	K	H	L	P	O	F	U
M	G	W	F	T	X	Z	Y	X
L	P	E	Q	K	D	Q	M	G
F	L	M	Y		G	Z		Y

1. What city did Joshua lead the children of Israel to
   march around?
2. Who helped the Israelite spies inside that city?
3. How many times did the children of Israel march
   around the city on the seventh day?
4. What did the people do after the seventh time,
   when the priests blew the trumpet?

23

WORD MATCH

Match the words with their definitions
by drawing lines to connect them.

1.	TARRY	1.	BELLY BUTTON
2.	SOLEMN	2.	DECORATE
3.	INHABIT	3.	SUPERVISORS
4.	KINSFOLKS	4.	RELATIVES
5.	NAVEL	5.	SERIOUS
6.	OVERSEERS	6.	WAIT
7.	PHARAOH	7.	LIVE THERE
8.	HOSEN	8.	PRETEND
9.	GARNISH	9.	KING OF EGYPT
10.	FEIGN	10.	GOWNS

TRUE or FALSE

		TRUE	FALSE
1.	Paul was a Saducee.	☐	☐
2.	All of Jacob's sons were very close and loved each other.	☐	☐
3.	Jesus called James and John "Sons of Thunder."	☐	☐
4.	Golgotha means "the place of the skeleton."	☐	☐
5.	Pilate tried to let Jesus go.	☐	☐
6.	Pharaoh let the Hebrew people go willingly.	☐	☐
7.	Even Job's wife did not comfort him.	☐	☐
8.	Judas Iscariot was greedy.	☐	☐
9.	Mary was still a virgin when Jesus was born.	☐	☐
10.	Nehemiah was sad because Jerusalem was in ruins.	☐	☐

CROSSWORD

ACROSS

  1. What a car is that's not new
  5. Like ice
  7. A laugh
  8. Abraham's birthplace (Gen. 11:31)
  9. Pretty ____ a picture
11. God's name for Himself, I ____ (Ex.3:14)
12. Note in the musical scale
13. Not a she but a ____
14. Get __ of that
16. Small rug
17. The land where Jeremiah lived (Jer. 1:1)
20. "He that refuseth reproof ____" (Prov. 10:17)
21. City in Syria where Paul traveled to (Acts 21:3)

DOWN

  1. Chaldean city (Neh. 9:7)
  2. The eternal part of a person
  3. Book of the Old Testament
  4. Delaware, abbr.
  5. "That food shall be for store to the land against the seven years of ____" (Gen. 41:36)
  6. One of the sons of Reuel (Gen. 36:13)

7. Land where God brought the Reubenites, near the river Gozan (1 Chron. 5:26)
10. Third son of Adam (Gen. 5:3)
15. ___ board
16. "Let me pull out the
    _____ out of thine eye" (Matt. 7:4)
18. Attempt
19. Not him

WORD SEARCH
MOTHERS IN THE BIBLE

After you've found all the words in the word search,
find all the unused letters in the puzzle. Unscramble
them to find the hidden words.

WORD LIST

ACHSAH

BATHSHEBA

BILHAH

DEBORAH

DINAH

EVE

HANNAH

JOCHABED

LEAH

MARY

NAIN

NOAH

PUAH

REBEKAH

RUTH

SARAH

SHUNAMITE

TAMAR

```
D S O H A N N A H S
I A D N L S D T H N
N R O E M E A U A B
A A A M B M N I I E
H H A O A A N L V H
E R R R M C H E B A
Y A S I U A H C D U
H E T L H T S S O P
R E B E K A H M A J
B A T H S H E B A H
```

WORD SCRAMBLES
NEW TESTAMENT BOOKS #2

1. ITUST _____

2. AMJSE _____

3. VRAOTNLEIE _____

4. NSSLIOCOSA _____

5. OTHTYIM _____

6. EPRTE _____

7. HANASEISTSLON _____

8. OEPIMNLH _____

9. DJEU _____

10. WSEHBER _____

11. SILNIHPIPPA _____

BIBLE TRIVIA

Did you know that
Moses wrote the
first five books of the Bible?

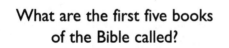

What are the first five books
of the Bible called?

CRYPT-CROSS

In xcu (14 down) beginning was the Word, and the Word was with God, and the Vbmw (1 down) was God. The jpqu (15 across) was in the furoiioir (13 across) with God. Pee (19 down) xcoirj (8 down) vumu (1 across) made fz (11 across) him; and voxcbkx (4 across) him was not piz (6 down) xcoir (10 across) qpwu (16 down) that was made. Oi (9 down) him was eohu (2 down); and the life was the eorcx (21 across) bh (20 across) qui (12 down). And the light jcoiuxc (7 down) in wpmsiujj (5 across); and the wpmsiujj (5 across) comprehended it ibx (18 down). There was a man sent from Rbw (3 down), whose name was tbci (17 across).

(JOHN 1:1-6)

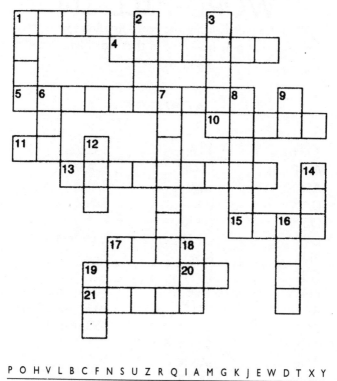

P O H V L B C F N S U Z R Q I A M G K J E W D T X Y

A B C D E F G H I J K L M N O P Q R S T U V W X Y Z

33

WORD-FILL-IN

Fill in the words using the word list. Start with the
words that only have one in that word length and
build around it.

WORD LIST

3 Letters
ANT
ASA
DAM
DEW
EAT
ERI
ITS
MAW
RAN
SAW
TEN
THE
VOW
WAX
WEB

4 Letters
EACH
EZRI
JAIR
MARA
OREB
RISE
SITH
TILE
VALE

5 Letters
JANNA
SNAIL

6 Letters
ELASAH
RAILER
RINSED

7 Letters
RAAMSES

10 Letters
ALEXANDRIA
CONSISTETH

11-LETTER ACROSTIC

Solve the clues for each word across.
The circled letter is the first letter of the next word.

1. Intoxication
2. Put in a good word for someone
3. Opened the understanding
4. Amused
5. What most children are guilty of at some time
6. The commander of Nebuchadnezzar's army
7. "...son of _____." (Num. 10:19)
8. A memorial
9. Places of ambush
10. Food
11. The width of a hand
12. His name looks like a laugh (1 Chr. 4:6)
13. The Jewish feast of booths
14. Slavedrivers
15. Filled up again
16. Jesus said this on the cross
17. A minister of state
18. Curses or untruths against God
19. People who try to make peace
20. "...blessings of my _____..." (Gen. 49:26)

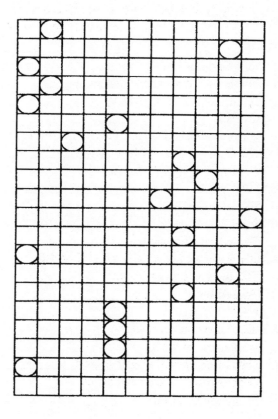

37

WORD SCRAMBLES
NEW TESTAMENT CHURCHES #1

1. SSEUHPE _____

2. PIIHLPPI _____

3. ELAJRMESU _____

4. HINATOC _____

5. AISAMAR _____

6. MERO _____

7. AAALGTI _____

8. SLHTASCAENOI _____

9. ARBEE _____

10. RNIOHCT _____

BIBLE CROSS OUTS

Cross off the letters that occur four times. The letters that are left will spell out the answers.

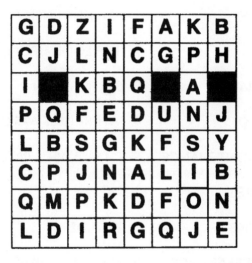

G	D	Z	I	F	A	K	B
C	J	L	N	C	G	P	H
I	■	K	B	Q	■	A	■
P	Q	F	E	D	U	N	J
L	B	S	G	K	F	S	Y
C	P	J	N	A	L	I	B
Q	M	P	K	D	F	O	N
L	D	I	R	G	Q	J	E

1. Who had to climb a tree to see Jesus because he was too short to see above the crowd?

2. What kind of a tree was it?

WORD MATCH

Match the words with their definitions by drawing
lines to connect them.

1. EDIFY		1. ESTHER'S ENEMY
2. FAIR		2. THE LOOK UPON A FACE
3. ANAKIMS		3. STRENGTHEN
4. BOOTY		4. WHERE JESUS WAS CRUCIFIED
5. COUNTENANCE		5. PUT UP WITH PATIENTLY
6. ERRED		6. PRETTY
7. DUMB		7. PLUNDER
8. FORBEARANCE		8. MADE A MISTAKE
9. GOLGOTHA		9. CANNOT SPEAK
10. HAMAN		10. GIANTS

TRUE or FALSE

TRUE   FALSE

1. Forty-two little children were
   mauled by bears for disrespectfully
   teasing Elisha about being bald.   ☐   ☐
2. Sodom was destroyed by hail.   ☐   ☐
3. The Apostle Peter denied that he
   even knew Jesus.   ☐   ☐
4. Immanuel means "God with us."   ☐   ☐
5. John the Baptist refused to baptize
   Jesus.   ☐   ☐
6. Samson ate honey out of the car-
   cass of a dead lion.   ☐   ☐
7. Rehoboam listened and followed
   wise advice.   ☐   ☐
8. The Apostle John was given the keys
   to the kingdom.   ☐   ☐
9. Balaam's donkey talked to him.   ☐   ☐
10. Nabal was glad to provide David
    and his men with food.   ☐   ☐

CROSSWORD

ACROSS

1. Big monkeys
5. "Let us run with _____ the race that is set before us" (Heb. 12:1)
9. Not off but ____
10. Some people thought Jesus was the reincarnation of this man (Matt. 16:14)
11. Short sleep times
13. Public Broadcasting Service, abbr.
14. Stop living
15. Continent where Jesus lived
16. Our enemy
18. New York, abbr.
19. "The whole _____ _____ sick, and the whole heart faint" (2 words) (Isa. 1:5)
21. Streams of light

DOWN

1. No one's _____ home
2. Desserts
3. Long, narrow fish
4. Uses scissors
5. Small lakes

6. "Shema, and ____" (Neh. 8:4)
7. Cottages
8. A nonfiction short writing
12. The disciple who walked on water
15. Boy's name
17. American Automobile Association, abbr.
20. "Greater ____ he that is in you" (1 John 4:4)

WORD SEARCH
RIVERS IN BIBLE LANDS

After you've found all the words in the word search,
find all the unused letters in the puzzle. Unscramble
them to find the hidden words.

WORD LIST

ABANA	MEJARKON
BESOR	NILE
CYRUS	PHARPAR
DANUBE	RHONE
DIYALA	SANGARIUS
DOURO	TIGRIS
JORDAN	UZAN
KARUN	ZARGA
LITANI	

```
U Z A N A D R O J N
E D G E L I N V O P
D A R O S E B K H D
I N A T I L R A O A
Y U Z B E A R U B C
A B I N J P R A R Y
L E O E A O N R E R
A H M R K A R U N U
R S U I R A G N A S
I S T I G R I S B L
```

BIBLE TRIVIA

Did you know that
there are thirty-nine books
in the Old Testament?

How many books
are in the whole Bible?

WORD SCRAMBLES
NEW TESTAMENT CHURCHES #2

1. TATRIHAY   _____

2. SAUDMSAC   _____

3. PAOJP   _____

4. CLIODAAE   _____

5. ALDYD   _____

6. NARYSM   _____

7. IAPLELAIHPDH   _____

8. ECARAASE   _____

9. MMEURAPG   _____

10. DISSRA   _____

CRYPT-CROSS

Wqtjgbkx (1 down), npkv (3 down) vnlb (16 down) zybkxma (14 across) tx (10 down) the jnbg (6 down): snb (17 down) this ta (8 down) bthqm (19 across). Honour mqv (15 down) symqkb (17 across) yxg (13 across) inmqkb (2 across); which is the first commandment with zbnitak (9 across); That tm (20 down) iyv (7 across) pk (4 down) well with mqkk (15 across), and mqnl (18 across) iyvkam (12 down) jtuk (5 across) long on the kybmq (11 down).   (EPHESIANS 6:1-3)

S R J Q W K D G M L E U T O X B H Z F I V Y C N A P
A B C D E F G H I J K L M N O P Q R S T U V W X Y Z

49

WORD-FILL-IN

Fill in the words using the word list. Start with the words that only have one in that word length and build around it.

WORD LIST

3 Letters
ERI
HAY
ICE
OWE
OWL

4 Letters
ELAM
ESLI
INTO
TOPS

5 Letters
GERAR
LIKED

6 Letters
APPAIM
ISHPAN

7 Letters
APELLES
JOKNEAM
OPENETH

8 Letters
EXACTETH
LONGEDST

9 Letters
ATTENTIVE

10 Letters
DELECTABLE

11 Letters
CANAANITISH

12 Letters
ESHKALONITES

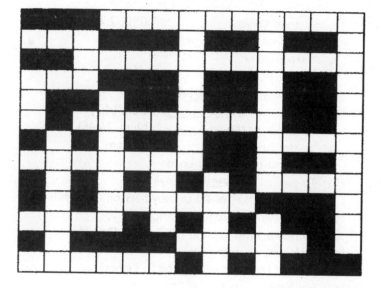

12-LETTER ACROSTIC

Solve the clues for each word across.
The circled letter is the first letter of the next word.

1. "...send to you _____..." (Phil. 2:25)
2. A long way of saying perhaps
3. A lawbreaker
4. Growing back
5. Pertaining to, Old English
6. "...that dwelt in _____." (Gen. 14:7)
7. "...family of the _____." (Num. 26:45)
8. "...the land of _____..." (2 Sam. 24:6)
9. Our gratitude to the Lord
10. To give an offering, Old English
11. What the Israelites did to baby boys on the eighth day
12. The Bible term for pregnancy
13. Someone who lived in the "city of David"
14. Bibletime shopping malls
15. One of Haman's sons (look in Esther)
16. frailness
17. The other Bible book that Jeremiah wrote
18. "..._____ the chamberlain..." (2 Kings 23:11)
19. "...Ephai the _____..." (Jer. 40:8)
20. "...deeds of the _____..." (Rev. 2:6)

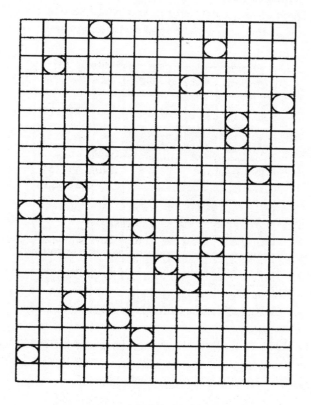

BIBLE CROSS OUTS

Cross off the letters that occur five times. The letters
that are left will spell out the answers.

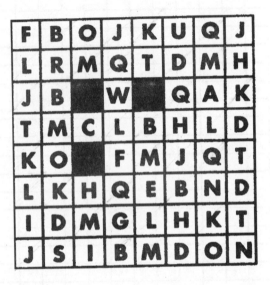

1. What time was it when Jesus walked on the water?

2. Who else walked on the water?

WORD MATCH

Match the words with their definitions by drawing
lines to connect them.

1.	HAUGHTY	1.	HANNAH'S RIVAL
2.	INNOCENT	2.	PROMISE
3.	JEZER	3.	CONCEITED
4.	KISHI	4.	NOT GUILTY
5.	LIBERTY	5.	ARGUMENT
6.	MAIL	6.	A SON OF NAPHTALI
7.	NARROW	7.	ARMOR
8.	OATH	8.	FATHER OF ETHAN
9.	PENINNAH	9.	THIN
10.	QUARREL	10.	FREEDOM

CROSSWORD

ACROSS

1. "He scattereth the _____-frost" (Ps. 147:16)
5. The opposite of lower
7. Set down
8. Neither
10. Establishment, abbr.
11. Not busy
12. One of Benjamin's sons (Gen. 46:21)
13. "Send ye the lamb to the ruler of the land from _____ to the wilderness" (Isa. 16:1)
14. "Let us slay him, and cast him into some ___" (Gen. 37:20)
15. _____, white, and blue
16. "The body is not one _____ but many" (1 Cor. 12:14)
19. What you plant

DOWN

1. "Israel dwelt among the _____" (Judg. 3:5)
2. One of the peoples destroyed by the Israelites (Josh. 2:10)
3. What you say when the doctor looks at your throat
4. "The recompence of a man's hands shall be _____ unto him" (Prov. 12:14)
5. Son of Dan (Gen. 46:23)
6. _____ skate

7. Chick's noise
9. _____ the book
11. Isaiah, abbr.
17. ___, myself, and I
18. _____ my valentine

WORD SEARCH
BOOKS OF THE BIBLE

After you've found all the words in the word search,
find all the unused letters in the puzzle. Unscramble
them to find the hidden words.

WORD LIST

ACTS
AMOS
CHRONICLES
EPHESIANS
EZRA
JAMES
JOB
JOEL
JOHN
JONAH

JOSHUA
JUDGES
MICAH
NAHUM
PETER
PSALMS
REVELATION
RUTH
SONG

```
O J C H A I L H R S
E O H A B C T E E P
P B R C L U T M V S
H Z O I R E A S E A
E A N M P J O G L L
S U I G M B D J A M
I H C N N U A O T S
A S L H J O H M I B
N O E O E K S A O S
S J S J O N A H N S
```

TRUE or FALSE

		TRUE	FALSE
1.	Saul was blinded by the brightness of Jesus' glory.	☐	☐
2.	Jesus got angry sometimes.	☐	☐
3.	The Lord told Moses to take his shoes off.	☐	☐
4.	The Roman soldiers broke Jesus' legs to make him die faster.	☐	☐
5.	Stephen was hanged for blasphemy.	☐	☐
6.	God sent the Egyptians darkness, but the Israelites had light.	☐	☐
7.	Nadab and Abihu were killed for offering strange fire.	☐	☐
8.	The cherubim guarded the garden of Eden with a flaming torch.	☐	☐
9.	Solomon asked God for great wealth.	☐	☐
10.	Luke and Mark are two of the twelve disciples.	☐	☐

WORD SCRAMBLES
OLD TESTAMENT BOOKS #2

1. OSGNFOLSOONMO   _____

2. ATEIECLSCSSE   _____

3. IOESRNHCLC   _____

4. VRSRBPOE   _____

5. IEEMNHAH   _____

6. ASMSLP   _____

7. HREETS   _____

8. ARZE   _____

9. BJO   _____

BIBLE TRIVIA

God told Noah to build:
a) a yacht for Christian cruises
b) an airplane
c) an ark
d) a tugboat

Did you know that
Noah's ark was 450 feet long?

BIBLE CROSS OUTS

Cross off the letters that occur four times. The letters that are left will spell out the answers.

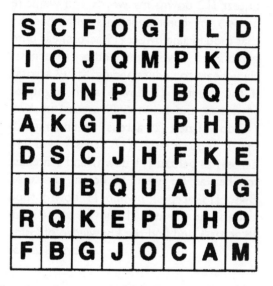

1. What was the name of David's wise son?

2. What was his mother's name?

3. What was his son's name?

CRYPT-CROSS

My pfc (17 down), if bwfq (2 across) wilt utjtezt (12 down) my words, and wemt (6 across) my commandments with thee; So that thou incline bwect (19 across) ear unto gepmfs (15 down), and nddhx (14 across) thine heart to understanding; Xtn (7 across), if thou juetpb (1 down) after acfghtmot (4 down), and hekbtpb (9 across) up bwx (18 down) zfejt (20 across) for understanding; If thou pttatpb (17 across) wtu (16 across) as pehztu (11 down), and searchest for her as for wem (3 down) treasures; Bwtc (13 across) pwnhb (5 down) thou understand the ktnu (10 down) of the hfum (8 across), and find the knowledge of God.

(PROVERBS 2:1-5)

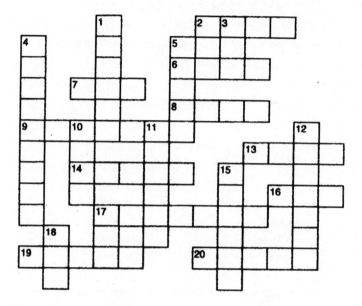

K T N P I O W L B C F Z D A G S U J M E R Q H Y X V
A B C D E F G H I J K L M N O P Q R S T U V W X Y Z

65

WORD-FILL-IN

Fill in the words using the word list. Start with the words that only have one in that word length and build around it.

WORD LIST

3 Letters
LIE

4 Letters
BANK
DREW
HARP

5 Letters
NEZIB

7 Letters
ASUNDER
COLLOPS
LIONESS
PROMOTE

9 Letters
AMBASSAGE
PERSUADED
WHOREDOMS

10 Letters
WORSHIPPED

11 Letters
CONTINUANCE
PREMEDITATE
SHOELATCHET

12 Letters
UNSEARCHABLE

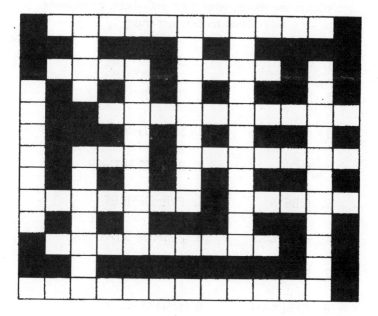

WORD MATCH

Match the words with their definitions by drawing
lines to connect them.

1.	LACK	1.	DIE
2.	LUSTS	2.	GOSSIP
3.	MALICE	3.	SOMETHING'S MISSING
4.	NON	4.	BOAZ'S FATHER
5.	OBEY	5.	EVIL DESIRES
6.	ODOURS	6.	JOSHUA'S FATHER
7.	PERISH	7.	EVIL INTENT
8.	REBEKAH	8.	SMELLS
9.	SALMA	9.	DO WHAT YOU'RE TOLD
10.	TALEBEARER	10.	ISAAC'S WIFE

WORD SCRAMBLES
NEW TESTAMENT CHURCHES #3

1. IAMTEL   _____

2. NAETSH   _____

3. RALSYT   _____

4. ASRTO   _____

5. ERTY   _____

6. YSCPRU   _____

7. HAIAAC   _____

8. CINMOIU   _____

9. EDBER   _____

10. AISYR   _____

CROSSWORD

ACROSS

1. Paddles
5. "Thou _____ them away as with a flood; they are as a sleep" (Ps. 90:5)
9. _____ upon a time
10. A kind of doctor's degree, abbr.
11. Chaplain, abbr.
12. When Abram pitched his tent, this city was to the east (Gen. 12:8)
13. Belonging to Shechem's father (Gen. 33:19)
15. Hurtful
16. Exclamation of triumph
18. A son of Benjamin (Gen. 46:21)
19. City built by Rehoboam (2 Chron. 11:5–6)
20. Certain

DOWN

1. Places where fruit trees grow
2. _____ you ready?
3. Rhode Island, abbr.
4. To divide something
5. Company, abbr.
6. Keeps a ship from drifting

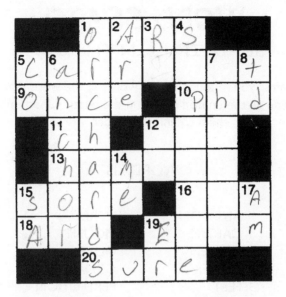

7. The father of scribes (1 Kings 4:3)
8. Touch down, abbr.
12. "_____, everyone that thirsteth" (Isa. 55:1)
14. _____, myself, and I
15. South America, abbr.
17. God told Moses His name was I _____
(Exod. 3:14)
19. Emergency room, abbr.

WORD SEARCH
BEAUTIFUL IN THE BIBLE

After you've found all the words in the word search,
find all the unused letters in the puzzle. Unscramble
them to find the hidden words.

WORD LIST

ABSALOM	LORD
CAPTIVE	MOUNT
DIADEM	OLIVE
ESTHER	ORNAMENT
FEET	PERFECTION
GARMENTS	RACHEL
HOUSE	ROD
JERUSALEM	TREE
KING	

```
C E V I L O D I J P
U A S T H O U S E T
A L P T R T R R R N
M B E T H E F D U E
E F S H I E E M S M
D B E A C V R O A A
A U L T L A E U L N
I K I N G O R N E R
D O T E E F M T M O
N A S T N E M R A G
```

CRYPT-CROSS

Ju (4 down) receive the instruction of wisdom, mryjahq (5 across), and judgment, and equity; To give yrkjafjl (2 across) to the simple, to the lurvb (1 down) man knowledge and discretion. A wise man will hear, and will avhcqpyq (20 across) learning; and a man of understanding shall pjjpav (13 down) rvju (9 down) wise hurvyqfy (8 down): To understand a proverb, and the interpretation; the tucgy (12 down) of the wise, and jdqac (15 across) dark sayings. The fear of the LORD is the kqbavvavb (10 across) of xvutfqgbq (11 across): krj (3 down) fools despise wisdom and instruction. My yuv (18 down), hear the instruction of thy npjdqc (16 across), and forsake vuj (21 across) the fpt (19 down) un (22 across) thy mother: For they shall be pv (17 down) ornament of bcphq (14 down) unto thy head, and chains about thy vqhx (7 across). My son, an (20 down) sinners entice thee, huvyqvj (6 down) thou not.

(PROVERBS 1:3-10)

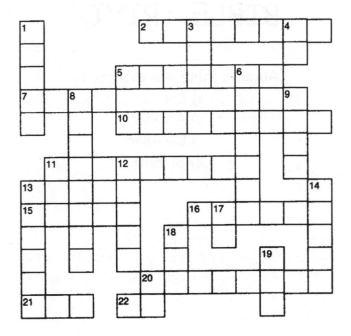

I G R H P L D C Q T B Y J F X A E U M W O N Z K S V
A B C D E F G H I J K L M N O P Q R S T U V W X Y Z

BIBLE TRIVIA

Abram's name was changed to:
- a) Lot
- b) Abraham
- c) Bam-Bam
- d) Brahma

Why did God change Abram's name?

BIBLE CROSS OUTS

Cross off the letters that occur seven times. The letters that are left will spell out the answers.

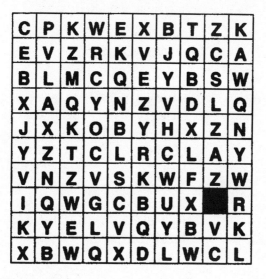

C	P	K	W	E	X	B	T	Z	K
E	V	Z	R	K	V	J	Q	C	A
B	L	M	C	Q	E	Y	B	S	W
X	A	Q	Y	N	Z	V	D	L	Q
J	X	K	O	B	Y	H	X	Z	N
Y	Z	T	C	L	R	C	L	A	Y
V	N	Z	V	S	K	W	F	Z	W
I	Q	W	G	C	B	U	X		R
K	Y	E	L	V	Q	Y	B	V	K
X	B	W	Q	X	D	L	W	C	L

1. Which three disciples went with Jesus to the high mountaintop?

2. What happened to Jesus there?

WORD-FILL-IN

Fill in the words using the word list. Start with the words that only have one in that word length and build around it.

WORD LIST

3 Letters
ALL
ANY
CIS
GIN
ITS
LOD
SUM
WHO

4 Letters
SHUR

5 Letters
DUKES
ERECH
LECAH
SIHOR

7 Letters
HUMBLED
MESSAGE
MIKLOTH

8 Letters
ENDAMAGE
STOODEST

10 Letters
EBEDMELECH

11 Letters
SHALLECHETH

12 Letters
KADESHBARNEA

13 Letters
MONEYCHANGERS
SWADDLINGBAND
UNDERSTANDEST

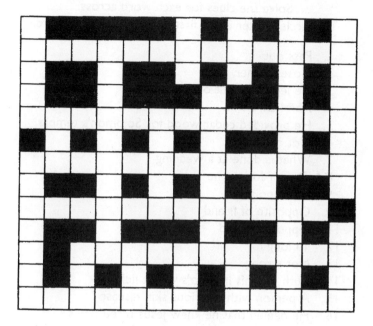

5-LETTER ACROSTIC

Solve the clues for each word across.
The circled letter is the first letter of the next word.

1. Pass out
2. Moses' father
3. He led Israel out of Egypt
4. Abraham's wife
5. He provided cedar wood for Solomon's temple
6. Not quite right
7. What is done at a wedding
8. The Jordon is one
9. Snake poison
10. Opposite of friend
11. Opposite of old
12. To long for
13. Not wrong
14. Ruth did this in Boaz's wheat field
15. A person with a serious skin disease
16. He denied that he knew Jesus three times
17. A shaving tool
18. A king of Israel who set the palace on fire while he was still in it
19. The tenth judge of Israel
20. The color of most wood

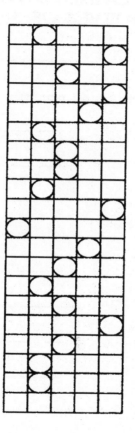

WORD SCRAMBLES
RELATIVES OF JESUS

1. RYMA _____

2. ESMAJ _____

3. TAHTMTA _____

4. DEJU _____

5. ETLAHSBIE _____

6. EHOSPJ _____

7. HLEIMC _____

8. NTIEPOASTJHBHT _____

9. EHIL _____

10. SHAIZARAC _____

WORD MATCH

Match the words with their definitions by drawing
lines to connect them.

1.	TEACH	1.	CONSUMING ENTHUSIASM
2.	TEMPEST	2.	GET CLEAN
3.	UNSHOD	3.	GROW
4.	UPBRAIDETH	4.	INSTRUCT
5.	VIGILANT	5.	BAREFOOT
6.	WASH	6.	STORM
7.	WAX	7.	WATCHFUL
8.	XERXES	8.	THROW IT IN YOUR FACE
9.	ZEBULUN	9.	ONE OF JACOB'S SONS
10.	ZEAL	10.	AHASUERUS

CROSSWORD

ACROSS

1. This man built a very large boat
5. "_____, Patrobas" (Rom. 16:14)
7. "_____, I come to do thy will" (Heb. 10:9)
8. Not a she
10. Editor, abbr.
11. Perfect
14. Gibeon was greater than this place (Josh. 10:2)
15. Shapes
16. Laugh noise
17. ___, myself, and I
18. "Children of _____" (Ezra. 2:42)
23. What you say to a baby when they shouldn't do something

DOWN

1. Nebraska, abbr.
2. Operating room, abbr.
3. I _____
4. Not she
5. Naham's sister (1 Chron. 4:19)
6. An Israelite (1 Chron. 7:37)
7. Jacob's first wife (Gen. 29:23)

9. You better do this or _____
11. "_____ it be thou, bid me come" (Matt. 14:28)
12. Accomplish
13. Emergency room, abbr.
19. Small word that comes before a noun beginning with a vowel
20. Give that _____ me
21. Not out
22. Turn over, abbr.

TRUE or FALSE

		TRUE	FALSE
1.	Moses and Elijah were on the mountain where Jesus was transfigured.	☐	☐
2.	Lydia was a seller of purple.	☐	☐
3.	Melchizedek was king of Jericho.	☐	☐
4.	Followers of Jesus were first called Christians in Jerusalem.	☐	☐
5.	Mary, Martha, and Lazarus lived in Capernaum.	☐	☐
6.	Gideon had 70 sons.	☐	☐
7.	Rachel and Leah got along very well.	☐	☐
8.	The poor widow gave more than the rich man.	☐	☐
9.	Hannah and Penninah got along very well.	☐	☐
10.	Eli thought Hannah was drunk in the sanctuary.	☐	☐

WORD SCRAMBLES
OLD TESTAMENT #3

1. LEEIEZK _____

2. INLDAE _____

3. EJIRHEAM _____

4. LJEO _____

5. HOJNA _____

6. SMAO _____

7. AISHIA _____

8. AMHIC _____

9. EAHSO _____

10. TMSITAONNAEL _____

WORD SEARCH
DAVID'S FAMILY

After you've found all the words in the word search,
find all the unused letters in the puzzle. Unscramble
them to find the hidden words.

WORD LIST

ABINADAB
ABISHAG
ABITAL
AMNON
BATHSHEBA
BOAZ
EGLAH
ELIAB

ELIADA
ELIPHELET
ELISHAMA
JESSE
KILEAB
NATHAN
OBED
ZERUIAH

```
Z E R U I A H A A R
K I L E A B O M N T
B O A Z B E A N A E
A B Y A I H A O H L
D A E B S S A N T E
A I G I H H D D A H
N L L T A T A E N P
I E A A G A I B L I
B T H L Y B L O K L
A J E S S E E I N E
```

BIBLE CROSS OUTS

Cross off the letters that occur four times. The letters
that are left will spell out the answers.

1. What did Jesus call the disciples James and John?

2. What did it mean?

3. What was their father's name?

WORD SCRAMBLES
PEOPLE INVOLVED IN GOLIATH'S DEFEAT

1. ADABBNAI _____

2. OLDR _____

3. RYAM _____

4. ERANB _____

5. ESJSE _____

6. BAEIL _____

7. IHGALOT _____

8. MASHHAM _____

9. ASLU _____

10. VIDDA _____

CRYPT-CROSS

Wherewithal shall a qaxft (3 down) osf (6 down) cleanse mgi (7 down) way? by taking heed emujuea (9 down) according to thy word. With my whole heart have I sought thee: O cue (4 down) me not wander zjao (10 down) thy commandments. Thy yajb (16 down) have I hid in ogfu (15 down) heart, that I ogtme (15 across) not igf (18 across) against thee. Pcuiiub (19 across) sje (1 down) emax (5 across), O LORD: teach me thy iesexeui (11 down). With my lips have I declared all emu (17 across) rxb-toufei (8 across) of thy oaxem (6 across). I have rejoiced in the way of emq (17 down) testimonies, as oxlm (14 across) as in all jglmui (12 down). I will meditate in thy njulunei (13 across), and have respect unto thy ways. I will delight oqiucz (2 across) in thy statutes: I will not forget thy word.   (PSALM 119:9-16)

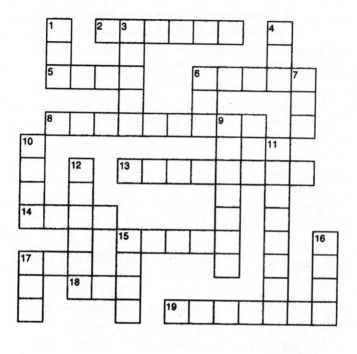

O D L Z T N I K S R X C H P M B Y J A G E Q V U W F
A B C D E F G H I J K L M N O P Q R S T U V W X Y Z

93

WORD-FILL-IN

Fill in the words using the word list. Start with the
words that only have one in that word length and
build around it.

WORD LIST

3 Letters
AGO
BAT
TEN

4 Letters
ARBA
AUNT

5 Letters
DEBIR
POLLS
RANGE
SPORT
ZEBAH

6 Letters
BRANCH
LOADEN

7 Letters
DIVORCE
THIEVES

8 Letters
GREATEST
HARBONAH
REBEKAHS

9 Letters
ASHURITES
DEFRAUDED

10 Letters
DESTROYETH

11 Letters
DETERMINATE

6-LETTER ACROSTIC

Solve the clues for each word across.
The circled letter is the first letter of the next word.

1. "...Amasa the son of _____..." (2 Chr. 28:12)
2. Opposite of big
3. Spoke
4. "...children of _____..." (Gen. 36:26)
5. Peter raised her from the dead
6. Hump-backed creatures
7. "..._____, to take..." (Jer. 36:26)
8. "..._____ the son..." (Num. 34:21)
9. "..._____ the Tekoite..." (2 Sam. 23:26)
10. To charge to one's account
11. Mistakes
12. Decayed
13. Something you shoot at
14. He went to heaven in a chariot drawn by horses of fire
15. Idols
16. The substance in your bones that makes blood
17. Elijah parted the Jordan river with this
18. Solomon built the first one
19. Jail
20. To hurt someone's feelings

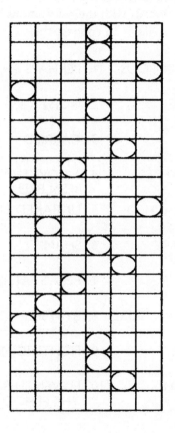

WORD MATCH

Match the words with their definitions by drawing
lines to connect them.

1. CLAMOUROUS	1. PERHAPS
2. BORNE	2. NOISY
3. BEOR	3. CARRIED
4. JACINTH	4. A COW THAT'S NEVER BEEN BRED
5. REPROACHED	5. UNBAKED BREAD
6. SOLITARY	6. SHAMED
7. SOLDIER	7. BELA'S FATHER
8. PERADVENTURE	8. BY ITSELF
9. HEIFER	9. FIGHTING MAN
10. DOUGH	10. ELEVENTH STONE ON THE EPHOD

BIBLE TRIVIA

Did you know that
the Hebrew word "Shaddai"
is the name used for God most often
in the Bible's early books?

Did you know that Shaddai means
"All Sufficient" or "Almighty"?

CROSSWORD

ACROSS

1. "Michmash, and _____" (Neh. 11:31)
5. "Be likeminded. . .being of one _____, of one mind"
   (Phil. 2:2)
7. "For they _____ evil against thee" (Ps. 21:11)
9. ___ you know what time it is?
10. Stand _____
11. What _____ you do?
13. Swallowed
14. Less than two
15. Made the earth
16. Angry feelings
19. "A bruised _____ shall he not break" (Isa. 42:3)

DOWN

1. To perform
2. Frozen water
3. Jonathan, for short
4. "Huppim, and ___" (Gen. 46:21)
5. To pour oil upon one
6. One who owes something
7. "Son of ___" (1 Kings 4:14)

8. What your hair is when it's not your natural color
12. Bambi was one
13. Grown older
17. ___, myself , and I
18. School class that involves the most physical exercise, abbr.

WORD SEARCH
SECRET THINGS IN THE BIBLE

After you've found all the words in the word search,
find all the unused letters in the puzzle. Unscramble
them to find the hidden words.

WORD LIST

BREAD	JOB
CHAMBERS	LOVE
ENTICED	MEN
FACES	NAME
FAULTS	PLACE
FEAR	PRESENCE
FLEE	SEARCH
GIFT	SPY
GOD	TABERNACLE
HEART	THINGS

```
F C H A M B E R S S
A E T R A E H T S J
C E N T I C E D G O
E E V O L N P G N B
S T L U A F L I I D
S P Y M D E A F H O
N E E L F A C T T G
E L C A N R E B A T
M E C N E S E R P E
C H C R A E S R B S
```

CRYPT-CROSS

Make a bnfgey (6 across) mnvrq (15 down) unto lzq (9 down) LORD, all ye lands. Rqwcq (14 down) the LORD with gladness: come before his twqrqmdq (19 across) with singing. Know ye that the ynws (10 across) he is hns (18 down): it is he lzxl (13 down) hath made us, and not we newrqycqr (7 down); we xwq (17 down) his people, xms (5 across) the sheep of his pasture. Enter into his hxlqr (12 down) with lzxmirhvcvmh (13 across), and vmln (3 down) his dnewlr (2 down) with praise: be thankful emln (8 across) him, and bless his name. For the LORD is good; his uqwdf (1 across) is qcqwyxrlvmh (16 across); and his lwelz (4 down) qmsewqlz (11 across) to all generations.   (Psalm 100:1-5)

104

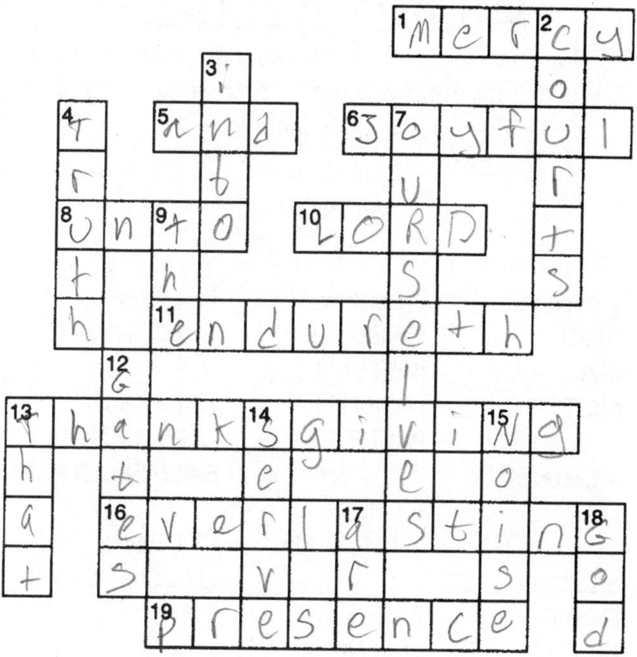

Q	J	V	C	U	Y	F	G	K	X	W	T	N	O	Z	B	E	S	D	P	M	I	R	A	L	H
A	B	C	D	E	F	G	H	I	J	K	L	M	N	O	P	Q	R	S	T	U	V	W	X	Y	Z

WORD-FILL-IN

Fill in the words using the word list. Start with the
words that only have one in that word length and
build around it.

WORD LIST

3 Letters
AGO
IRA
NOT

4 Letters
LEHI

5 Letters
DRIVE
NAOMI
STOOL

7 Letters
CHERITH
INSTEAD
JACINTH
PALTITE

8 Letters
SHIPHTAN

9 Letters
LEVITICAL
SLANDERED

10 Letters
TROUBLEDST

11 Letters
OPPOSITIONS

12 Letters
DISPUTATIONS
EVILMERODACH

13 Letters
ELELOHEISRAEL

WORD SCRAMBLES
STONES ON THE EPHOD

1. MEYATHTS _____

2. YXNO _____

3. AEGAT _____

4. ESJRAP _____

5. ODDAMIN _____

6. LYBER _____

7. ZTOPA _____

8. BLEARCCUN _____

9. DSURSIA _____

10. AHIJTCN _____

11. DEELRAM _____

12. IPSHRAEP _____

TRUE or FALSE

1. Jesus told Peter to pay their taxes with a fish. ☐ ☐
2. Elijah was fed by frogs by the brook Cherith. ☐ ☐
3. The Apostle Paul survived a deadly snakebite. ☐ ☐
4. Jonah's vine was eaten by a bird. ☐ ☐
5. Daniel was thrown into the fiery furnace. ☐ ☐
6. Leah was a shepherdess. ☐ ☐
7. God created birds on the fifth day. ☐ ☐
8. Noah took 7 of each kind of bird on the ark. ☐ ☐
9. When Moses struck the rock, bread came out. ☐ ☐
10. Paul was from the city of Ephesus originally. ☐ ☐

BIBLE CROSS OUTS

Cross off the letters that occur four times. The letters
that are left will spell out the answers.

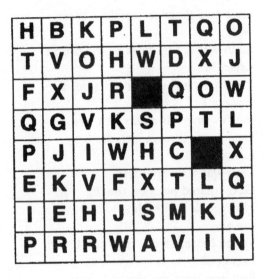

H	B	K	P	L	T	Q	O
T	V	O	H	W	D	X	J
F	X	J	R		Q	O	W
Q	G	V	K	S	P	T	L
P	J	I	W	H	C		X
E	K	V	F	X	T	L	Q
I	E	H	J	S	M	K	U
P	R	R	W	A	V	I	N

1. Name the first five plagues that the Lord brought
   to the Egyptians through Moses.

110

WORD SCRAMBLES
THE APOSTLES

1. TWHATME _____

2. MSJAE _____

3. HRWOEATMOLB _____

4. ETPRE _____

5. NERWAD _____

6. HSTOMA _____

7. UASDJ _____

8. ONJH _____

9. NOSIM _____

10. ULAP _____

11. IPHPLI _____

CRYPT-CROSS

Now faith cb (8 down) the bljbqtdug (10 across) of things wangm (9 down) for, qwg (13 across) evidence ah (11 across) things daq (3 down) seen. For by cq (20 down) the gvmgeb (15 across) ajqtcdgm (7 down) a good egnaeq (6 across). Qwealyw (13 down) faith zg (14 across) understand that the zaevmb (14 down) zgeg (5 down) het-igm (17 across) by the zaem (5 across) of God, ba (4 down) qwtq (1 across) things which teg (2 down) bggd (21 across) were not itmg (18 down) of qwcdyb (19 across) zwcuw (12 across) ma (16 down) appear.

(HEBREWS 11:1-3)

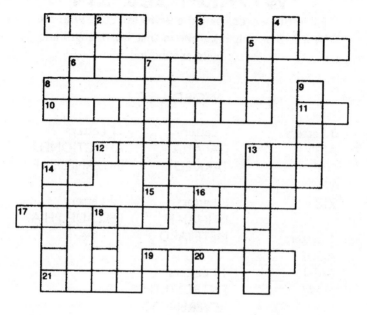

O S I N R J E F M B X U D P K V T Z Y A C L H Q G W
A B C D E F G H I J K L M N O P Q R S T U V W X Y Z

113

WORD-FILL-IN

Fill in the words using the word list. Start with the
words that only have one in that word length and
build around it.

WORD LIST

3 Letters
APT
SPY
YES
ZIZ

4 Letters
AGUE
BANI
MAAI

6 Letters
KAREAH

7 Letters
GALATIA
TARRIED

8 Letters
ISHMAIAH
METEYARD

10 Letters
ENTREATETH
REVERENCED
TRIUMPHING

11 Letters
AFFECTIONED
INTERMEDDLE

12 Letters
PHILADELPHIA

BIBLE CROSS OUTS

Cross off the letters that occur five times. The letters
that are left will spell out the answers.

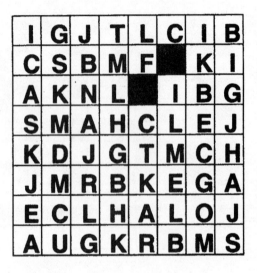

1. What were Jesus' last words on the cross?

2. How long did the darkness last while Jesus was on
   the cross?

WORD SCRAMBLES
PEOPLE & THINGS IN THE GARDEN

1. OHNISP   _____

2. IBSRD   _____

3. AMDA   _____

4. HOING   _____

5. LEDDEIHK   _____

6. TESNRPE   _____

7. AIASLMN   _____

8. TSUEEHAPR   _____

9. ESTER   _____

10. VEE   _____

CROSSWORD

ACROSS

1. Long, long ____
4. Michigan Institute of Technology, abbr.
7. A gate (2 Kings 11:6)
8. A son of Gad (Gen. 46:16)
9. "Which maketh ____, Orion, and Pleiades, and the chambers of the south" (Job 9:9)
12. "Lest he ____ thee to the judge" (Luke 12:58)
13. Kemuel's son (Gen. 22:21)
14. "____, and Zabad" (Ezra 10:27)
18. Not new
19. I stubbed my big ____
20. It is, contraction
21. "Mount ____" (Num. 20:25)

DOWN

1. "____ did that which was right in the eyes of the Lord" (1 Kings 15:11)
2. "Up to ____" (2 Kings 9:27)
3. Places where fruit trees grow
4. "Hand of ____" (Ezra 8:33)
5. A son of Caleb (1 Chron. 4:15)
6. "My Country ____ of Thee"

10. "Straightway the spirit ____ him" (Mark 9:20)
11. "Of ___" (1 Chron. 7:17)
14. Write quickly
15. This man took care of Samuel in the temple
16. Also
17. Not his

WORD-FILL-IN

Fill in the words using the word list. Start with the
words that only have one in that word length and
build around it.

WORD LIST

3 Letters	5 Letters	8 Letters
ITS	ALPHA	FINISHER
NOB	LINUS	
NOT		9 Letters
RIB	6 Letters	REVOLTING
	LEBANA	
4 Letters	SCRAPE	11 Letters
AGUE		ABELMIZRAIM
ANON	7 Letters	
ARZA	BABBLER	12 Letters
HOLE	DRESSER	ABOMINATIONS
RAIN	HUSBAND	
READ	REACHED	13 Letters
		STRENGTHENING

BIBLE CROSS OUTS

Cross off the letters that occur four times. The letters that are left will spell out the answers.

F	C	J	O	E	M	R	K
L	T	P	Q	Y	B	U	D
K	M	A	C	J	Y	E	P
S	Q	B	A	M	L	N	B
U	D	E	J	F	K	Q	O
	L	R	C	P	T	U	B
Y	K	U	N	Q	J	I	L
C	G	E	P	H	M	T	S

1. How many days and nights did the rain come while Noah and his family were on the ark?

122

WORD MATCH

Match the words with their definitions by drawing
lines to connect them.

1.	ITHRA	1.	CONTROL
2.	MASCHIL	2.	CRIED
3.	MASONS	3.	JAMES' AND JOHN'S FATHER
4.	PALACE	4.	A DIDACTIC POEM
5.	REPENTANCE	5.	STONE WORKERS
6.	REND	6.	AMASA'S FATHER
7.	SNARE	7.	A CHANGE OF MIND
8.	TAME	8.	TEAR
9.	WEPT	9.	TRAP
10.	ZEBEDEE	10.	A KING'S HOUSE

7-LETTER ACROSTIC

Solve the clues for each word across.
The circled letter is the first letter of the next word.

1. This bird can't fly
2. Light producing wax sticks
3. Refuse
4. Babies
5. A hard reach
6. Languages
7. "...Jeshua, and _____..." (Ezra 8:33)
8. Countries
9. Often, Old English
10. The Philistines made gold ones to send back with the captured ark
11. The number of years the Israelites spent in Babylon
12. Psalm 22 foretells the casting of lots on this
13. He has two New Testament books with his name
14. To receive something when someone dies
15. A burglary
16. What a gossip repeats, Old English spelling
17. We get our groceries at super_____
18. Abraham's wife after Sarah died

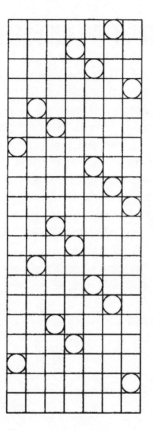

19. Started a fire
20. A place of torture in a prison

125

CRYPT-CROSS

Jesus answered, If I honour ofuinv (15 across), my kqeqly (17 across) is eqjkbez (7 down): it is my vmjkiy (11 down) that kqeqlyijk (1 across) me; of whom ye umf (4 across), that he is your God: Yet ye have not known him; but I know him: and if I should say, I know him not, I ukmnn (14 down) be a liar like unto you: but I know kbo (12 across), and keep his saying. Your father Abraham yisqbx-ir (9 across) to uii (10 across) my day: and he saw it, and was glad. Then said the Jews unto him, Thou myj (18 across) not yet fifty years qnr (2 down), mer (16 across) hast thou uiie (14 across) Abraham? Jesus said unto them, Verily, ciybnf (8 down), I say unto fql (5 down), hivqyi (13 down) Abraham was, I am. Then jqqp (3 down) they up ujqeiu (4 down) to cast at him: but Jesus hid kbouinv (1 down), and went qlj (6 across) of the jiowni (19 across), going through the obruj (15 down) of them, and so passed by.

(JOHN 8:54-59)

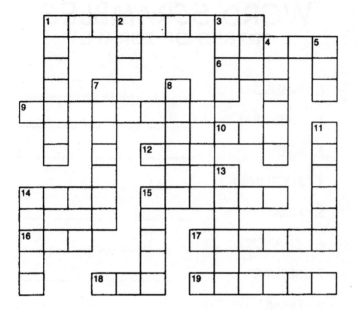

Q I V W N Y Z B E T H U A L M K O D J X S F P C R G
A B C D E F G H I J K L M N O P Q R S T U V W X Y Z

WORD SCRAMBLES
TRIBES OF ISRAEL

1. NMEISO   _____

2. CASHSRAI   _____

3. ILVE   _____

4. EULZUNB   _____

5. NDA   _____

6. AHANLIPT   _____

7. BERUNE   _____

8. DHAJU   _____

9. HAEMANSS   _____

10. IEAMRPH   _____

11. NJMBEINA   _____

12. ADG   _____

BIBLE CROSS OUTS

Cross off the letters that occur four times. The letters that are left will spell out the answers.

B	J	O	M	I	P	L	G
Q	S	W	V	H	A	V	P
I	V	L	J	G	■	L	M
W	O	■	C	Q	U	W	S
Q	G	T	P	S	■	D	W
A	M	R	K	J	N	V	E
J	S	S	Q	F	I	M	R
S	P	T	B	O	G	R	N

1. Name the last five plagues that the Lord brought to the Egyptians through Moses.

WORD SCRAMBLES
WORKS OF THE FLESH

1. RMSRDEU   _____

2. LUSYJEOA   _____

3. DAYREULT   _____

4. RSEFTI   _____

5. HTRAW   _____

6. CTIFCRTWAH   _____

7. SSLNECNAEUN   _____

8. ICANOTROFIN   _____

9. ENNDUNKSRES   _____

10. RHAEDT   _____

11. IGNREESVL   _____

12. TOADRYLI   _____

13. VSNIYENG   _____

BIBLE CROSS OUTS

Cross off the letters that occur five times. The letters
that are left will spell out the answers.

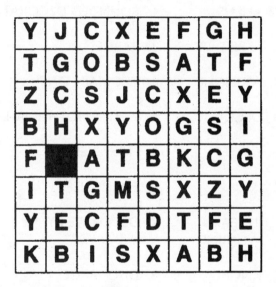

Y	J	C	X	E	F	G	H
T	G	O	B	S	A	T	F
Z	C	S	J	C	X	E	Y
B	H	X	Y	O	G	S	I
F		A	T	B	K	C	G
I	T	G	M	S	X	Z	Y
Y	E	C	F	D	T	F	E
K	B	I	S	X	A	B	H

1. Name the three sons of King Josiah who were
   kings of Judah.

WORD MATCH

Match the words with their definitions by drawing
lines to connect them.

1. ALIENS

2. ALBEIT

3. ASUNDER

4. DECK

5. FLOTES

6. ISSUE

7. JUDEA
   WEARING

8. KNOP

9. NAOMI

10. PRINCIPAL

1. ROUNDED DECORATIVE
   PARTS

2. BARGES

3. THE MAIN ONE

4. RUTH'S MOTHER-IN-LAW

5. HOWEVER

6. FOREIGNERS

7. DECORATE BY

8. DISCHARGE

9. THE SOUTHERN
   PART OF JUDAH

10. APART

BIBLE CROSS OUTS

Cross off the letters that occur six times. The letters
that are left will spell out the answers.

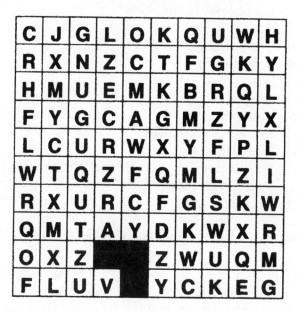

C	J	G	L	O	K	Q	U	W	H
R	X	N	Z	C	T	F	G	K	Y
H	M	U	E	M	K	B	R	Q	L
F	Y	G	C	A	G	M	Z	Y	X
L	C	U	R	W	X	Y	F	P	L
W	T	Q	Z	F	Q	M	L	Z	I
R	X	U	R	C	F	G	S	K	W
Q	M	T	A	Y	D	K	W	X	R
O	X	Z			Z	W	U	Q	M
F	L	U	V		Y	C	K	E	G

1. Who baptized Jesus?
2. What was the sign he saw to let him know who
   Jesus was?

133

CROSSWORD

ACROSS

1. To prepare food
5. The opposite of remember
7. Not well
8. "Pispah, and ___" (1 Chron. 7:38)
10. Opposite of yes
11. Exist
13. Uruguay, abbr.
14. Turn over, abbr.
15. Emergency room, abbr.
16. South America, abbr.
17. "To him that _____ his conversation aright will I shew the salvation of God" (Ps. 50:23)
20. "So shall they be _____ pained at the report of Tyre" (Isa. 23:5)
21. Menahem's father (2 Kings 15:14)

DOWN

1. Colossians, abbr.
2. Operating room, abbr.
3. Biblical king (1 Kings 4:19)
4. "Shoa, and ____" (Ezek. 23:23)
5. Things that you walk on

6. Reliable
7. Divide _____ two pieces
9. "Ulla; _____" (1 Chron. 7:39)
11. Son of Zophah (1 Chron. 7:37)
12. Made a mistake
18. A faithful pet
19. Priest that Samuel stayed with in the temple (1 Sam. 2:11)

WORD SEARCH
WIVES IN THE BIBLE

After you've found all the words in the word search,
find all the unused letters in the puzzle. Unscramble
them to find the hidden words.

WORD LIST

AHIMOAM   KETURAH
BAARA   LEAH
BILHAH   MARY
EGLAH   MICHAL
EVE   NAOMI
HAGAR   ORPAH
HODESH   PENINNAH
HUSHIM   RUTH
JAEL   SARAH
JOANNA

```
F E A H I M O A M A
M R V K E T U R A H
L J A E O B H H U U
B A O G A J A E L S
I Y H A A N L E A H
L R R C N H G H S I
H A W I I N E A R M
A M N I V M A P U O
H E H A R A S R T A
P E S H S E D O H N
```

CRYPT-CROSS

The LORD is my ruvbuvwm (19 across); I shall jyg (9 across) want. He maketh me to xkv (12 down) down in dwvvj (4 down) pastures: he leadeth me beside the rgkxx (6 across) ilgvwr (1 down). He restoreth my soul: he leadeth me in guv (5 down) paths of righteousness for ukr (17 down) name's sake. Fvl (18 down), guyodu (13 down) I walk through the slxxvf (3 down) of the shadow of death, I will cvlw (14 across) no evil: cyw (14 down) thou lwg (20 across) ikgu (2 down) me; guf (5 across) rod and thy staff guvf (10 down) comfort me. Thou bwvblwvrg (8 down) a glzxv (13 across) before me in the presence of mine enemies: thou anointest my uvlm (15 down) with oil; my cup wojjvgu (16 across) over. Rowvxf (11 across) goodness and mercy shall follow me all the days of my life: and I will dwell in the house of the LORD for vsvw (7 across). (PSALM 23:1-6)

M P F G C Y T X W N I A D Q U J Z S V K H E R L O B
A B C D E F G H I J K L M N O P Q R S T U V W X Y Z

139

WORD-FILL-IN

Fill in the words using the word list. Start with the
words that only have one in that word length and
build around it.

WORD LIST

3 Letters
ATE
NOE
SAP
TWO

4 Letters
ROWS
URGE

5 Letters
EPHAH
RANGE

7 Letters
MINDING

8 Letters
JEHOAHAZ
QUIETETH

9 Letters
IDOLATERS
NEGLIGENT
PASSOVERS

10 Letters
EVANGELIST
FOURSQUARE
TARPELITES

11 Letters
CONTENTMENT

12 Letters
STOUTHEARTED

WORD SCRAMBLES
FRUIT OF THE SPIRIT

1. RYEMC   _____

2. SGEODNSO   _____

3. KSNEESEM   _____

4. TEANPIEC   _____

5. EEPAC   _____

6. YJO   _____

7. HFTAI   _____

8. ORLCELSNFTO   _____

9. NSSIEDNK   _____

10. ESNNGELTES   _____

11. VEOL   _____

BIBLE CROSS OUTS

Cross off the letters that occur four times. The letters
that are left will spell out the answers.

C	K	E	M	Q	L	J	F
I	N	S	P	G	T	H	M
Q	A	C	J	Z	N	Q	B
F	T	I	K	T	L	F	S
D	N	S	A	T	M	D	G
K	Z	C	J	O	N	S	P
H	M	A	Q	R	G	E	K
L	G	I	F	H	J	C	U

1. Name the four friends of Job who gave him counsel.

143

WORD-FILL-IN

Fill in the words using the word list. Start with the
words that only have one in that word length and
build around it.

WORD LIST

3 Letters
OUT

4 Letters
ARMS
DIRT
DOGS
LAID
OBIL
SUSI

6 Letters
HILLEL
SCHOOL

7 Letters
NISROCH
STILLED

8 Letters
CHILIONS
REHABIAH

9 Letters
ESTEEMING
GOLDSMITH

10 Letters
SEARCHINGS

11 Letters
MAGISTRATES

12 Letters
ASTONISHMENT

13 Letters
MALICIOUSNESS
THESSALONIANS

CROSSWORD

ACROSS
1. Saul's new name after he saw Christ
5. Women carry these
7. Still
8. Machine used for carding cotton
10. Operating room, abbr.
11. God told Moses to tell Pharaoh that I ____ had sent him (Exod. 3:14)
13. Opposite of yes
14. "Men of ____" (Jer. 48:31)
17. Priest who was with Samuel in the temple (1 Sam. 1:17)
18. Be in debt
19. Used for seasoning foods
22. Seth's son (Gen. 5:6)

DOWN
1. ____ the dishes on the table
2. Arkansas, abbr.
3. Ourselves
4. A limb used for walking
5. Dangers

6. "I will lay _____ upon you" (Ezek. 37:6)
7. Joins two work animals
9. Used to smell
11. Open up and say _____
12. _____, myself and I
15. Fruit that is no longer green
16. More than one roe
20. Not out
21. Company, abbr.

WORD SCRAMBLES
OLD TESTAMENT BOOKS #4

1. RCELSNHOCI _____

2. GGIAHA _____

3. GNSIK _____

4. ALHIAMC _____

5. SLAEUM _____

6. EZHICAARH _____

7. ANMHU _____

8. HPZAHIANE _____

9. UKKKHBAA _____

BIBLE CROSS OUTS

Cross off the letters that occur four times. The letters
that are left will spell out the answers.

F	C	J	I	K	M	V	G
L	E	P	W	T	Q	B	H
Q	M	O	G	L	U	J	P
S	C	K	A	M	W	N	B
W	D	L	B	F	C	Q	O
P	G	U	Q	J	R	K	W
T	M	H	O	P	G	U	L
J	S	B	A	N	K	C	D

1. How many men did Jesus feed each time he fed the
   multitudes?

WORD-FILL-IN

Fill in the words using the word list. Start with the words that only have one in that word length and build around it.

WORD LIST

3 Letters
BEG
CUD
IRA
THE

4 Letters
AHER
GIAH
OAKS
SUSI

5 Letters
HOOKS
PELET
RITES

8 Letters
CONFUSED

10 Letters
PRESIDENTS
SLANDERETH

11 Letters
BANQUETINGS

12 Letters
ALLONBACHUTH

13 Letters
BETHMARCABOTH
DETERMINATION
RIGHTEOUSNESS
TRANSGRESSORS

WORD SEARCH
BABIES IN THE BIBLE

After you've found all the words in the word search,
find all the unused letters in the puzzle. Unscramble
them to find the hidden words.

WORD LIST

ABEL	JOSEPH
ASHER	JUDAH
DAN	LEVI
EPHRAIM	OBED
GAD	PEREZ
ISAAC	SAMUEL
ISSACHAR	SETH
JESUS	SIMEON
JOASH	ZEBULUN

```
B P S P H P E S O J
N E I L S C A A S I
U R M E E B O I A R
L E E V T U S B E I
U Z O I H S M H E A
B N N S A S S A E D
E S A C D A G I S A
Z O H D J E S U S B
J A E P H R A I M E
R C E L J U D A H L
```

B P B A I A S S I C E L

BABIES

153

BIBLE CROSS OUTS

Cross off the letters that occur four times. The letters
that are left will spell out the answers.

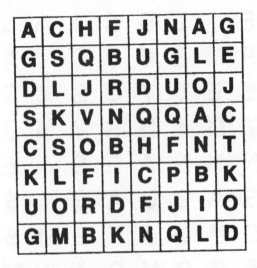

A	C	H	F	J	N	A	G
G	S	Q	B	U	G	L	E
D	L	J	R	D	U	O	J
S	K	V	N	Q	Q	A	C
C	S	O	B	H	F	N	T
K	L	F	I	C	P	B	K
U	O	R	D	F	J	I	O
G	M	B	K	N	Q	L	D

1. Who was Esther's husband?
2. Who was his first wife?
3. What was the name of the Jewish holiday that
   happened in the book of Esther?

154

WORD MATCH

Match the words with their definitions by drawing
lines to connect them.

1. SOJOURNER	1. MINERAL POTASH
2. TARES	2. BETHLEHEM
3. PARCEL	3. DORCAS
4. NITRE	4. ETHIOPIA
5. NOE	5. TRAVELER
6. GAD	6. WEEDS
7. EPHRATAH	7. SLAVERY
8. TABITHA	8. GREEK FORM OF NOAH
9. CUSH	9. ONE OF JACOB'S SONS
10. BONDAGE	10. A PORTION OF LAND

WORD SEARCH
BROTHERS IN THE BIBLE

After you've found all the words in the word search,
find all the unused letters in the puzzle. Unscramble
them to find the hidden words.

WORD LIST

ABEL	JOAB
ABISHAI	JOKSHAN
CAIN	JONATHON
DAVID	LAHMI
ELIAB	NAHOR
ESAU	SAPH
HARAN	SETH
ISAAC	SIPPAI
ISHMAEL	

```
I E H A R A N I T B
N S I L E A M H S I
A A A B B H P A S J
H U H A A A S R O R
S C S L C I O N R D
K A I E P H A J I H
O I B P A T A V T B
J N A N H B A E O I
L I A O E D S L R H
E S N L E E L I A B
```

8-LETTER ACROSTIC

Solve the clues for each word across.
The circled letter is the first letter of the next word.

1. Time to eat
2. Embroidered carpet
3. The early Americans wanted independence because of this
4. Fruit groves
5. Hand rails on stairs
6. One of Jacob's sons by Bilhah
7. The Jewish holiday remembering the night of deliverance from Egypt
8. Towards the East
9. Tortures
10. Laws
11. The twelfth foundation of the new Jerusalem
12. Another title for a pastor
13. To keep something the same
14. "...Benhadad, the son of _____..." (1 Kings 15:18)
15. Solomon's son
16. Jacob and Esau were this
17. "...Raamah, and _____..."(1 Chr. 1:9)
18. horse drawn war carts
19. "...the other _____." (1 Kings 7:20)
20. Birds with beautiful tail feathers

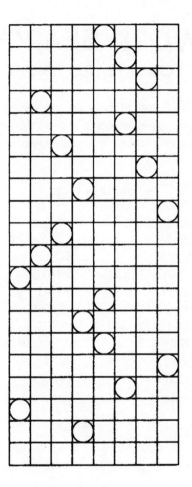

159

WORD SEARCH
JOB'S HARD TRIAL

After you've found all the words in the word search,
find all the unused letters in the puzzle. Unscramble
them to find the hidden words.

WORD LIST

BILDAD	POTSHERD
BOILS	ROBE
DAUGHTERS	SHAVED
DUST	SONS
ELIHU	SWORD
ELIPHAZ	WEPT
FIRE	WHIRLWIND
GOD	WIFE
LORD	WIND
OXEN	

```
S W O R D O G L S A
W D R E H S T O P D
I H R E L I P H A Z
F R I O D J T U O U
E I B R L A G N X H
D U S T L H D B E I
E S F P T W O L N L
B O I E O I I J I E
O N R W L D A N O B
R S E S H A V E D Y
```

9-LETTER ACROSTIC

Solve the clues for each word across.
The circled letter is the first letter of the next word.

1. Garbage piles
2. Someone born in Israel
3. Jesus makes us this way when we obey the Gospel
4. Decorated
5. Very effective
6. People from Egypt
7. Something that can be put up with
8. Herod's Temple was made up of several of these
9. Workers, Old English
10. "...daughter of _____" (1 Kings 15:2)
11. What happens at weddings
12. Where the Jews worshipped other than the Temple
13. What happens if you need your appendix out
14. To make up after a disagreement
15. Practised
16. Sincerely
17. To make bigger, Old English
18. Something that takes place without apparent effort
19. A custom that is handed down through the generations
20. Pays attention to, Old English

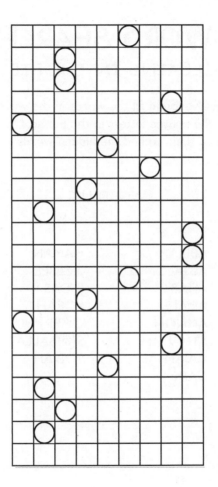

WORD SEARCH
VILLAINS IN THE BIBLE

After you've found all the words in the word search,
find all the unused letters in the puzzle. Unscramble
them to find the hidden words.

WORD LIST

ABIRAM

ABSALOM

AHAB

AMALEK

AMNON

ATHALIAH

CAIAPHAS

CAIN

HAMAN

JEZEBEL

JUDAS

KORAH

OMRI

SANBALLAT

TOBIAH

```
A A S I U E N A D S
T A A R D G B I S N
H M D M N S T A A G
A N U O A O N L H C
L O J L B B E A P M
I N O I A B A H A N
A M A L E K A R I B
H H L Z A R I Y A D
M A E B O B S H C A
T J L K A N A M A H
```

BIBLE CROSS OUTS

Cross off the letters that occur four times. The letters
that are left will spell out the answers.

L	F	A	J	C	Z	G	A
O	R	P	U	Q	K	S	I
M	G	A	C	R	O	P	Y
J	A	O	N	F	D	K	G
Q	I	M	J	A	C	R	T
H	F	K	A	P	B	I	Q
P	E	C	Q	T	■	H	J
G	K	A	I	O	N	F	Y

1. Who did Jesus raise up from the dead after four
   days in the grave?

2. What were his sisters' names?

3. Where did they live?

BIBLE CROSS OUTS

Cross off the letters that occur five times. The letters that are left will spell out the answers.

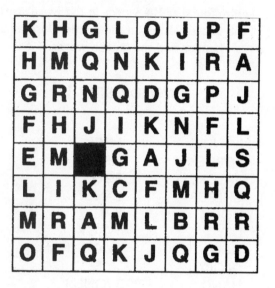

1. What were the names of Eli's sons?

2. What was the name of Eli's grandson who was born when his father was killed in battle?

167

WORD SEARCH
EZEKIEL'S VISIONS

After you've found all the words in the word search,
find all the unused letters in the puzzle. Unscramble
them to find the hidden words.

WORD LIST

BONES
BORDER
CALDRON
CHERUB
DOOR
DRY
GATE
GLORY
HAND
INCENSE

LOCK
MEAT
ROD
SANCTUARY
SINEWS
WAIST
WATCHMAN
WIFE
WOMEN

```
E Y N S H E F I W G
I S R A I T S I A W
G N N A M N A T D L
L D O E U H E E S N
O O E R C T C W M E
R O M K D N C T S M
Y R D R K L I N A O
B U R E H C A D A W
Z B O N E S O C E S
B O R D E R A L E E
```

BIBLE CROSS OUTS

Cross off the letters that occur five times. The letters
that are left will spell out the answers.

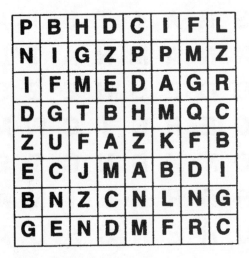

P	B	H	D	C	I	F	L
N	I	G	Z	P	P	M	Z
I	F	M	E	D	A	G	R
D	G	T	B	H	M	Q	C
Z	U	F	A	Z	K	F	B
E	C	J	M	A	B	D	I
B	N	Z	C	N	L	N	G
G	E	N	D	M	F	R	C

1. Where were Paul and Silas in jail together?

2. What happened when they sang praises to God at
   midnight?

3. Who was converted to faith in Christ because of
   this?

170

SOLUTIONS

Let's see how you did. . .

WORD MATCH

Pg. 5	Pg. 24	Pg. 40	Pg. 55	Pg. 68
1. 10	1. 6	1. 3	1. 3	1. 3
2. 6	2. 5	2. 6	2. 4	2. 5
3. 5	3. 7	3. 10	3. 6	3. 7
4. 2	4. 4	4. 7	4. 8	4. 6
5. 8	5. 1	5. 2	5. 10	5. 9
6. 3	6. 3	6. 8	6. 7	6. 8
7. 9	7. 9	7. 9	7. 9	7. 1
8. 7	8. 10	8. 5	8. 2	8. 10
9. 4	9. 2	9. 4	9. 1	9. 4
10. 1	10. 8	10. 1	10. 5	10. 2

Pg. 83	Pg. 98	Pg. 123	Pg. 132	Pg. 155
1. 4	1. 2	1. 6	1. 6	1. 5
2. 6	2. 3	2. 4	2. 5	2. 6
3. 5	3. 7	3. 5	3. 10	3. 10
4. 8	4. 10	4. 10	4. 7	4. 1
5. 7	5. 6	5. 7	5. 2	5. 8
6. 2	6. 8	6. 8	6. 8	6. 9
7. 3	7. 9	7. 9	7. 9	7. 2
8. 10	8. 1	8. 1	8. 1	8. 3
9. 9	9. 4	9. 2	9. 4	9. 4
10. 1	10. 5	10. 3	10. 3	10. 7

TRUE or FALSE

<u>Pg. 13</u> 1. FALSE - It was Goliath's son who had six of each. 2. FALSE - He sent a raven out first. 3. TRUE 4. TRUE 5. FALSE - It was 5,000 with 5 loaves and 2 fishes 6. TRUE 7. FALSE - It was the Red Sea.
8. FALSE - He was beheaded. 9. FALSE - This was a trick question. The Bible doesn't say what kind of fruit it was. 10. TRUE

<u>Pg. 25</u> 1. FALSE - He was a Pharisee. 2. FALSE - They were very jealous of Joseph. 3. TRUE 4. FALSE - It means the place of the skull. 5. TRUE
6. FALSE - We all know that story. 7. TRUE 8. TRUE 9. TRUE 10. TRUE

<u>Pg. 41</u> 1. TRUE 2. FALSE - It was fire and brimstone. 3. TRUE 4. TRUE
5. FALSE - He felt unworthy, but obeyed the Lord. 6. TRUE 7. FALSE - It was because he didn't listen that Israel became divided. 8. FALSE - It was Peter. 9. TRUE 10. FALSE - Nabal didn't like David even though David had helped him.

<u>Pg. 60</u> 1. TRUE 2. TRUE 3. TRUE 4. TRUE 5. FALSE - He was stoned to death. 6. TRUE 7. TRUE 8. FALSE - It was a sword. 9. FALSE - He asked for wisdom. God gave him wealth, too, because his heart was right.
10. FALSE - They weren't part of the twelve.

<u>Pg. 86</u> 1. TRUE 2. TRUE 3. FALSE - It was Salem. 4. FALSE - It was Antioch. 5. FALSE - It was Bethany. 6. TRUE 7. FALSE - They were jealous of each other. 8. TRUE 9. FALSE - Penninah made fun of Hannah because she couldn't have children. 10. TRUE

<u>Pg. 109</u> 1. TRUE - The fish had a coin in its mouth. 2. FALSE - It was ravens.
3. TRUE 4. FALSE - It was a worm. 5. FALSE - It was his friends. 6. FALSE - It was Rachel. 7. TRUE 8. TRUE 9. FALSE - It was water.
10. FALSE - It was Tarsus.

WORD SCRAMBLES

Pg. 3 1. CURTAINS 2. LAMPSTAND 3. ALTAR 4. INCENSE 5. VEIL
6. GATE 7. TABLE 8. ARK 9. OIL 10. LAVER

Pg. 8 1. ACTS 2. LUKE 3. EPHESIANS 4. ROMANS 5. CORINTHIANS
6. JOHN 7. GALATIANS 8. MARK 9. MATTHEW

Pg. 12 1. WIVES 2. FEMALES 3. MALES 4. SHEM 5. FOWL 6. HAM
7. JAPHETH 8. BEASTS 9. CATTLE 10. NOAH

Pg. 15 1. JUDGES 2. NUMBERS 3. DEUTERONOMY 4. EXODUS
5. KINGS 6. GENESIS 7. LEVITICUS 8. JOSHUA 9. RUTH 10. SAMUEL

Pg. 22 1. JOASH 2. AZARIAH 3. DAVID 4. AMAZIAH 5. JOTHAM
6. JEHOSHAPHAT 7. JOSIAH 8. SOLOMON 9. HEZEKIAH 10. ASA
11. UZZIAH

Pg. 30 1. TITUS 2. JAMES 3. REVELATION 4. COLOSSIANS
5. TIMOTHY 6. PETER 7. THESSALONIANS 8. PHILEMON 9. JUDE
10. HEBREWS 11. PHILIPPIANS

Pg. 38 1. EPHESUS 2. PHILIPPI 3. JERUSALEM 4. ANTIOCH 5. SAMARIA
6. ROME 7. GALATIA 8. THESSALONICA 9. BEREA 10. CORINTH

Pg. 47 1. THYATIRA 2. DAMASCUS 3. JOPPA 4. LAODICEA 5. LYDDA
6. SMYRNA 7. PHILADELPHIA 8. CAESAREA 9. PERGAMUM 10. SARDIS

Pg. 61 1. SONG OF SOLOMON 2. ECCLESIASTES 3. CHRONICLES
4. PROVERBS 5. NEHEMIAH 6. PSALMS 7. ESTHER 8. EZRA 9. JOB

Pg. 69 1. MELITA 2. ATHENS 3. LYSTRA 4. TROAS 5. TYRE 6. CYPRUS
7. ACHAIA 8. ICONIUM 9. DERBE 10. SYRIA

<u>Pg. 82</u> 1. MARY 2. JAMES 3. MATTHAT 4. JUDE 5. ELISABETH
6. JOSEPH 7. MELCHI 8. JOHN THE BAPTIST 9. HELI 10. ZACHARIAS

<u>Pg. 87</u> 1. EZEKIEL 2. DANIEL 3. JEREMIAH 4. JOEL 5. JONAH
6. AMOS 7. ISAIAH 8. MICAH 9. HOSEA 10. LAMENTATIONS

<u>Pg. 91</u> 1. ABINADAB 2. LORD 3. ARMY 4. ABNER 5. JESSE 6. ELIAB
7. GOLIATH 8. SHAMMAH 9. SAUL 10. DAVID

<u>Pg. 108</u> 1. AMETHYST 2. ONYX 3. AGATE 4. JASPER 5. DIAMOND
6. BERYL 7. TOPAZ 8. CARBUNCLE 9. SARDIUS 10. JACINTH
11. EMERALD 12. SAPPHIRE

<u>Pg. 111</u> 1. MATTHEW 2. JAMES 3. BARTHOLOMEW 4. PETER
5. ANDREW 6. THOMAS 7. JUDAS 8. JOHN 9. SIMON 10. PAUL
11. PHILIP

<u>Pg. 117</u> 1. PISHON 2. BIRDS 3. ADAM 4. GIHON 5. HIDDEKEL
6. SERPENT 7. ANIMALS 8. EUPHRATES 9. TREES 10. EVE

<u>Pg. 128</u> 1. SIMEON 2. ISSACHAR 3. LEVI 4. ZEBULUN 5. DAN
6. NAPHTALI 7. REUBEN 8. JUDAH 9. MANASSEH 10. EPHRAIM
11. BENJAMIN 12. GAD

<u>Pg. 130</u> 1. MURDERS 2. JEALOUSY 3. ADULTERY 4. STRIFE 5. WRATH
6. WITCHCRAFT 7. UNCLEANNESS 8. FORNICATION
9. DRUNKENNESS 10. HATRED 11. REVELINGS 12. IDOLATRY
13. ENVYINGS

<u>Pg. 142</u> 1. MERCY 2. GOODNESS 3. MEEKNESS 4. PATIENCE
5. PEACE 6. JOY 7. FAITH 8. SELF CONTROL 9. KINDNESS
10. GENTLENESS 11. LOVE

<u>Pg. 148</u> 1. CHRONICLES 2. HAGGAI 3. KINGS 4. MALACHI
5. SAMUEL 6. ZECHARIAH 7. NAHUM 8. ZEPHANIAH 9. HABAKKUK

CROSSWORD

Pg. 6

A	R	A	B		E	A	R
B	A	B	E		Z	I	T
S	W	I	N	G	E	R	S
			G		O	K	
A	G	A	G		I	I	I
D	R	I	P	P	E	R	S
A	I	L			E	L	O	N
M	T		W	A	S	N	O

Pg. 26

		U	S	E	D		
	F	R	O	Z	E	N	
H	A		U	R		A	S
A	M		I	A		H	E
R	I	D			M	A	T
A	N	A	T	H	O	T	H
	E	R	R	E	T	H	
		T	Y	R	E		

Pg. 42

		A	P	E	S		
P	A	T	I	E	N	C	E
O	N		E	L	I	A	S
N	A	P	S		P	B	S
D	I	E		A	S	I	A
S	A	T	A	N		N	Y
	H	E	A	D	I	S	
		R	A	Y	S		

Pg. 56

		H	O	A	R		
	H	I	G	H	E	R	
P	U	T			N	O	R
E	S	T		I	D	L	E
E	H	I		S	E	L	A
P	I	T		R	E	D	
	M	E	M	B	E	R	
		S	E	E	D		

Pg. 70

Pg. 84

Pg. 100

Pg. 118
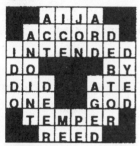

Pg. 134

Pg. 146

177

BIBLE TRIVIA

<u>Pg. 14</u>
EVE

<u>Pg. 46</u>
SIXTY-SIX

<u>Pg. 31</u>
PENTATEUCH

<u>Pg. 62</u>
C.) AN ARK

<u>Pg.76</u>
B.) ABRAHAM
Because He had promised to make him the father of many nations.

178

BIBLE CROSS OUTS

WORD SEARCH

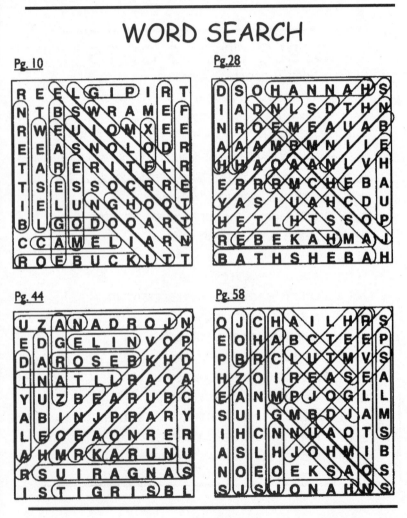

Pg. 10

Pg. 28

Pg. 44

Pg. 58

Pg. 72

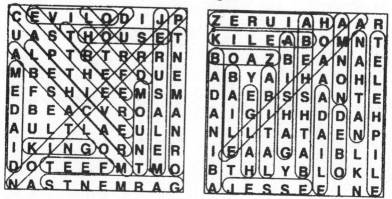

Pg. 88

Pg. 103

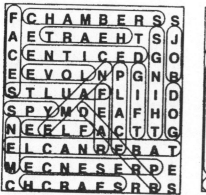

Pg. 136

Pg. 152

Pg. 156

Pg. 160

Pg.164

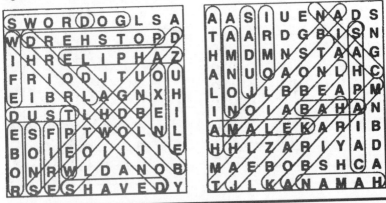

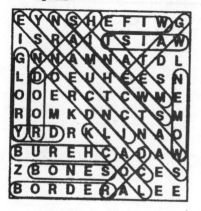

CRYPT-CROSS

Pg.16 ACTS 2:37-42

Pg.32 JOHN 1:1-6

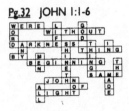

Pg.48 EPH. 6:1-3

Pg.64 PROV. 2:1-5

Pg.74 PROV. 1:3-10

Pg.92 PSA. 119:9-16

184

Pg.104 PSA. 100

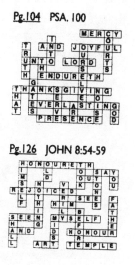

Pg.112 HEB. 11:1-3

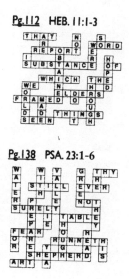

Pg.126 JOHN 8:54-59

Pg.138 PSA. 23:1-6

WORD-FILL-IN

Pg.18

Pg.34

Pg.50

Pg.66

Pg.78

Pg.94

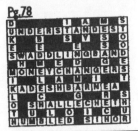

Pg.106

ELELOHEISRAEL
DISPUTATIONS
STOOL
CHERITH
NAOMI PALTITE
NOT DRIVE
LEHI INSTEAD

Pg.114

PHILADELPHIA
REVERENCED
TARRIED
GALATIA
INTERMEDDLE
AGUE ISHMAIAH

Pg.120

DRESSER
LEBANA NOB ARZA
HOLE
LINUS
FINISHER ALPHA
BABBLER NOT
ABOMINATIONS

Pg.140

SAP
CONTENTMENT
TWO
EPHAH
RANGE
QUIETETH URGE
PASSOVERS
EVANGELIST

Pg.144

MALICIOUSNESS
MAGISTRATES
ASTONISHMENT
THESSALONIANS
GOLDSMITH
LAID NISROCH
DOGS

Pg.150

BETHMARCABOTH
PRESIDENTS
ALLONBACHUTH
DETERMINATION
RIGHTEOUSNESS
TRANSGRESSORS

ACROSTIC

Pg. 20

R	I	N	G	L	E	A	D	E	R
G	R	U	D	G	I	N	G	L	Y
L	E	F	T	H	A	N	D	E	D
F	O	R	E	I	G	N	E	R	S
E	I	G	H	T	E	E	N	T	H
T	A	L	E	B	E	A	R	E	R
A	B	O	M	I	N	A	B	L	E
M	A	T	T	I	T	H	I	A	H
M	A	N	S	E	R	V	A	N	T
R	E	C	O	M	P	E	N	S	E
O	P	P	R	E	S	S	I	O	N
E	A	R	T	H	Q	U	A	K	E
E	N	G	R	A	V	I	N	G	S
N	E	I	G	H	B	O	U	R	S
R	E	F	R	E	S	H	E	T	H
F	A	I	T	H	F	U	L	L	Y
L	I	K	E	M	I	N	D	E	D
N	E	E	D	L	E	W	O	R	K
K	I	R	I	A	T	H	A	I	M
K	O	R	A	T	H	I	T	E	S

Pg. 36

D	R	U	N	K	E	N	N	E	S	S
R	E	C	O	M	M	E	N	D	E	D
E	N	L	I	G	H	T	E	N	E	D
E	N	T	E	R	T	A	I	N	E	D
N	A	U	G	H	T	I	N	E	S	S
N	E	B	U	Z	A	R	A	D	A	N
Z	U	R	I	S	H	A	D	D	A	I
R	E	M	E	M	B	R	A	N	C	E
A	M	B	U	S	H	M	E	N	T	S
N	O	U	R	I	S	H	M	E	N	T
H	A	N	D	B	R	E	A	D	T	H
H	A	A	H	A	S	H	T	A	R	I
T	A	B	E	R	N	A	C	L	E	S
T	A	S	K	M	A	S	T	E	R	T
R	E	P	L	E	N	I	S	H	E	D
S	A	B	A	C	H	T	H	A	N	I
C	H	A	M	B	E	R	L	A	I	N
B	L	A	S	P	H	E	M	I	E	S
P	E	A	C	E	M	A	K	E	R	S
P	R	O	G	E	N	I	T	O	R	S

188

```
E P A P H R O D I T U S
P E R A D V E N T U R E
T R A N S G R E S S O R
R E G E N E R A T I O N
A P P E R T A I N E T H
H A Z E Z O N T A M A R
M A L C H I E L I T E S
J A H T I M H O D S H I
T H A N K F U L N E S S
S A C R I F I C E D S T
C I R C U M C I S I N G
C H I L D B E A R I N G
B E T H L E H E M I T E
M A R K E T P L A C E S
P A R S H A N D A T H A
D E L I C A T E N E S S
L A M E N T A T I O N S
N A T H A N M E L E C H
N E T O P H A T H I T E
N I C O L A I T A N E S
```

```
F A I N T
A M R A M
M O S E S
S A R A H
H I R A M
A M I S S
M A R R Y
R I V E R
V E N O M
E N E M Y
Y O U N G
Y E A R N
R I G H T
G L E A N
L E P E R
P E T E R
R A Z O R
Z I M R I
I B Z A N
B R O W N
```

189

```
H A D L A I
L I T T L E
T A L K E D
D I S H O N
D O R C A S
C A M E L S
A B D E E L
E L I D A D
I K K E S H
I M P U T E
E R R O R S
R O T E N
T A R G E T
E L I J A H
I M A G E S
M A R R O W
M A N T L E
T E M P L E
P R I S O N
O F F E N D
```

```
O S T R I C H
C A N D L E S
D E C L I N E
I N F A N T S
S T R E T C H
T O N G U E S
N O A D I A H
N A T I O N S
O F T I M E S
E M E R O D S
S E V E N T Y
V E S T U R E
T I M O T H Y
I N H E R I T
R O B B E R Y
R U M O U R S
M A R K E T S
K E T U R A H
K I N D L E D
D U N G E O N
```

```
M E A L T I M E
T A P E S T R Y
T A X A T I O N
O R C H A R D S
R A I L T N G S
N A P H A L I I
P A S S O V E R
E A S I W A R D
T O R M E N T S
S T A T U T E S
A M E T H Y S T
M I N I S T E R
M A I N T A I N
T A B R I M O N
R E H O B O A M
B R O T H E R S
S A B T E C H A
C H A R I O T S
C H A P I T E R
P E A C O C K S
```

```
D U N G H I L L S
I S R A E L I T E
R I G H T E O U S
G A R N I S H E D
E F F E C T U A L
E G Y P T I A N S
T O L E R A B L E
B U I L D I N G S
L A B O U R E R S
A B I S H A L O M
M A R R I A G E S
S Y N A G O G U E
O P E R A T I O N
R E C O N C I L E
R E H E A R S E D
E A R N E S T L Y
E N L A R G E T H
N A T U R A L L Y
T R A D I T I O N
R E G A R D E T H
```

COLOR *the* PICTURE

LET'S FOLLOW JESUS

SOME DAYS LIFE CAN BE REALLY TOUGH. WE CAN HAVE PROBLEMS AT SCHOOL, WITH OUR FREINDS, AT HOME, AND EVEN WITH OUR PARENTS.

SOME DAYS WE CAN FEEL REALLY ANGRY OR AFRAID OR HURT OR LONELY — AND THAT'S ONLY A FEW OF THE FEELINGS WE WILL EXPERIENCE AS WE GROW THROUGH LIFE.

SO WHAT DO WE DO? HOW DO WE HANDLE ALL OUR FEELINGS? HOW DO WE HANDLE THE PROBLEMS THAT CAN COME AND BRING UP THESE FEELINGS IN US?

DO WE HAVE A CHOICE IN HOW WE CAN HANDLE OUR PROBLEMS AND FEELINGS?

YES! THERE IS A WAY: IF WE TURN TO GOD AND ASK HIM FOR HELP, HE CAN TEACH US HOW TO HANDLE SITUATIONS THAT WILL LEAD US TO HAVE HAPPIER LIVES.

IT'S A BETTER WAY, IF WE FOLLOW JESUS.

LET'S FIND OUT HOW!

"I AM THE LIGHT OF THE WORLD. WHOEVER FOLLOWS ME WILL NEVER WALK IN DARKNESS, BUT WILL HAVE THE LIGHT OF LIFE."

JOHN 8:12

WORD SEARCH

FEELINGS, FEELINGS—EVERYWHERE ARE FEELINGS!

FIND THE FEELINGS LISTED BELOW IN THE WORD SEARCH ON THE NEXT PAGE.

JOY

HURT

LOVE

ANGER

HATRED

FEAR

LONELINESS

PRIDE

GUILT

PEACE

HAPPINESS

WORRY

196

```
H R Q L Y V D M F K F W
F J G O N C L G P E F B
G S J V B T B X B W A L
A D B E B D F L X O T R
P N T P E L Q S C R F D
T P G R B W C X U R S X
R Z T E B V D H V Y S G
W A C T R B D M D M E W
H A P P I N E S S P N L
Q L R V B J D Z B D I D
M W I B B P E K C F L Q
B Y D N B C T W T H E J
T C E P A Q N S N K N W
N M J E B V S M Q B O P
K R P D B R D G U I L T
```

197

FILL *in the* BLANKS

SO MANY FEELINGS, SO MANY PROBLEMS. GOOD TIMES, BAD TIMES. HAPPINESS, DISAPPOINTMENT. IT'S CONFUSING! HOW DO YOU COPE—HOW DO YOU SORT IT ALL OUT?

LOOK TO GOD AND REALLY PUT YOUR TRUST IN **HIM**. NOT ONLY WILL YOU HAVE A GUARANTEE OF HEAVEN ONE DAY, BUT **HE** WILL HELP YOU RIGHT NOW AND IN EVERY DAY AHEAD!

GRACE
CONFIDENCE
TIME
APPROACH
RECEIVE

THRONE
HELP
MERCY
NEED

USING THE WORDS ABOVE, COMPLETE THE VERSE ON THE NEXT PAGE.

"LET US THEN _____
THE _____ OF GRACE WITH
_____, SO THAT WE MAY
_____ _____ AND FIND
_____ TO _____ US IN OUR
_____ OF _____."

HEBREWS 4:16

199

SCRAMBLED VERSES

WHAT DID JESUS SAY?

UNSCRAMBLE THE VERSE BELOW AND
COMPLETE THE NEXT PAGE TO READ JESUS'
OWN WORDS TO YOU!

"EOCM OT EM, LAL OYU OWH REA
YWRAE NAD DNEEBRUD, DAN I LILW
EGVI UYO ETSR. ETKA YM YEKO PNUO
UYO NAD RLNAE MFOR EM, RFO I MA
NTGELE DNA MUHLBE NI ARTHE,
ADN UOY LIWL IDFN SRTE OFR ROYU
SSLUO. RFO MY KYEO SI SYAE DAN
MY UDBERN SI ITLGH."

MATTHEW 11:28-30

201

SECRET CODES

JESUS SAVES!

TO SOLVE THE CODED VERSE BELOW, LOOK AT EACH LETTER AND WRITE THE ONE THAT COMES BEFORE IT IN THE ALPHABET.

"GPS UIF XBHFT PG TJO JT EFBUI,

CVU UIF HJGU PG HPE JT FUFSOBM

MJGF JO DISJTU KFTVT PVS MPSE."

202

ABCDEFGHIJKLMNOPQRS
TUVWXYZ

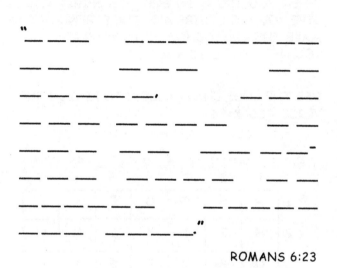

"___ ___ ___ ___ ___   ___ ___ ___   ___ ___ ___ ___
___ ___   ___ ___ ___   ___ ___   ___ ___
___ ___ ___ ___ ___,   ___ ___ ___
___ ___ ___ ___ ___ ___ ___   ___ ___
___ ___ ___   ___ ___   ___ ___ ___ ___-
___ ___ ___   ___ ___ ___ ___   ___ ___ ___
___ ___ ___ ___ ___   ___ ___ ___ ___
___ ___ ___   ___ ___ ___ ___."

ROMANS 6:23

203

FINISH *the* VERSE

NEW LIFE!

WHEN YOU TRUST IN GOD, HIS SPIRIT WILL
GIVE YOU THE DESIRE AND THE STRENGTH TO
MAKE THE RIGHT CHOICES IN YOUR LIFE. ALL
YOU NEED TO DO IS ASK HIM!

USE THE CODE CHART BELOW TO FINISH THE
VERSE. (EG: K=24)

	1	2	3	4	5	6	7
1	A	B	C	D	E	F	G
2	H	I	J	K	L	M	N
3	O	P	Q	R	S	T	U
4	V	W	X	Y	Z		

"SO I __ __ __ , __ __ __ __
      35 11 44   25 22 41 15

BY THE __ __ __ __ __ __ , AND
       35 32 22 34 22 36

YOU   __ __ __ __   NOT
             42 22 25 25

__ __ __ __ __ __ __
17 34 11 36 22 16 44

__ __ __ __ __ __ __   OF   THE
14 15 35 22 34 15 35

__ __ __ __ __ __   __ __ __ __ __ __ ."
35 22 27 16 37 25   27 11 36 37 34 15

GALATIANS 5:16

205

FILL THEM IN

FRUIT OF THE SPIRIT

LOOK UP GALATIANS 5:22-23 IN YOUR BIBLE.

ON THE NEXT PAGE, FILL IN THE BOXES WITH
THE FRUIT OF THE SPIRIT.

206

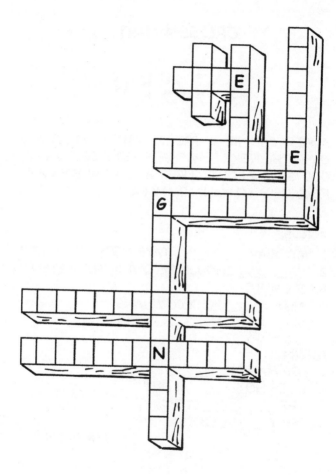

CROSSWORD

ANGER

ANGER CAN BE A PRETTY AWFUL FEELING.
OVER THE NEXT FEW PAGES, LET'S SEE WHAT
GOD SAYS ABOUT ANGER AND HOW WE CAN
FIND HELP TO HANDLE ANGER.

ACROSS

1. "MY DEAR _____, TAKE NOTE OF THIS."
2. "_____ SHOULD BE QUICK TO LISTEN."
3. "SLOW TO _____."
4. "AND _____ TO BECOME ANGRY."

DOWN

1. "FOR MAN'S _____."
2. "DOES NOT _____ ABOUT."
3. "THE _____ LIFE."
4. "THAT ___ DESIRES."

JAMES 1:19-20

208

209

DOUBLE *the* FUN

UNSCRAMBLE THE UNDERLINED WORDS IN EACH VERSE. ON THE NEXT PAGE, PLACE YOUR ANSWERS IN THE SPACES PROVIDED AND THEN COMPLETE THE CROSSWORD PUZZLE.

1. "IN YOUR ANGER DO NOT SIN; WHEN YOU ARE ON YOUR DESB, SEARCH YOUR ATRHSE AND BE SILENT."

PSALM 4:4

2. "FOR HIS ENARG LASTS ONLY A TMOENM, BUT HIS FAVOR LASTS A LIFETIME."

PSALM 30:5

3. "YET HE WAS MERCIFUL; HE VROEAFG THEIR INIQUITIES AND DID NOT DESTROY THEM. TIME AFTER MEIT HE RESTRAINED HIS ANGER AND DID NOT STIR UP HIS FULL TWHRA."

PSALM 78:38

1. _ _ _ _   _ _ _ _ _ _

2. _ _ _ _ _   _ _ _ _ _ _

3. _ _ _ _ _ _ _   _ _ _ _

    _ _ _ _ _

MULTIPLE CHOICE

ANGER IS JUST A FEELING, BUT IT IS WHAT YOU DO WITH IT THAT CAN MAKE IT RIGHT OR WRONG.

1. YOUR BROTHER CALLS YOU A NAME. WHAT SHOULD YOU DO?
   - A) CALL HIM AN EVEN NASTIER NAME.
   - B) TELL HIM THAT WASN'T NICE AND THAT YOU DIDN'T LIKE IT.
   - C) IGNORE HIM AND DON'T SPEAK TO HIM AGAIN.

2. YOU WANT TO STAY OVERNIGHT AT A FRIEND'S HOUSE. YOUR PARENTS SAY NO.
   - A) YOU SHOULD ARGUE WITH THEM.
   - B) YOU SHOULD HAVE A TEMPER TANTRUM.
   - C) YOU SHOULD ACCEPT THEIR ANSWER AND MAKE OTHER PLANS.

3. A FRIEND SHARES HER CANDY WITH EVERYONE ELSE, BUT LEAVES YOU OUT.
   - A) CALL HER NAMES.
   - B) TALK ABOUT HER BEHIND HER BACK.
   - C) TELL HER PRIVATELY HOW YOU FEEL.

4. JUST BEFORE IT'S YOUR TURN IN THE HOT DOG LINE, SOMEONE BUTTS IN FRONT OF YOU.

    A) YELL AT THEM AND TELL THEM YOU'RE NEXT.

    B) POLITELY TELL THEM YOU ARE NEXT.

    C) PUSH THEM OUT OF THE WAY.

5. THE TEACHER EMBARRASSES YOU IN FRONT OF THE CLASS.

    A) TALK POLITELY WITH THE TEACHER AFTER CLASS.

    B) EMBARRASS THE TEACHER BACK.

    C) AFTER CLASS, PUT TACKS ON THE TEACHER'S CHAIR.

6. YOU SEE A GROUP OF KIDS PICKING ON YOUR FRIEND.

    A) RUN IN WITH FISTS FLYING.

    B) GO TO AN ADULT FOR HELP.

    C) GO STAND BESIDE YOUR FRIEND.

FILL THEM IN

ACTS OF THE SINFUL NATURE

LOOK UP GALATIANS 5:19-21 IN YOUR BIBLE.

ON THE NEXT PAGE, FILL IN THE BOXES WITH THE SINFUL ACTS.

214

SCRAMBLED VERSES

UNSCRAMBLE THE VERSES BELOW, THEN
COMPLETE THE NEXT PAGE.

"NI UYRO GEANR OD TNO NSI: OD
NTO TLE HET SNU OG WDNO HLIEW
OYU EAR LTLIS AYGRN, DAN OD TON
EIGV ETH LDVEI A HFTLOODO."
EPHESIANS 4:26-27

"TGE DRI FO LAL NSSETBTIRE, ERGA
NDA GNARE, WGRBLAIN DAN AER-
SNLD, NLAGO IWHT RYVEE MFRO FO
MIALEC. EB IDKN DAN NAPIOOMTC-
SAES OT EON HTRAENO, IIFVRGONG
CHAE EOHRT, SJTU SA NI HTCIRS
DGO GRFOEVA OYU."
EPHESIANS 4:31-32

216

FINISH *the* VERSE

USE THE CODE CHART BELOW TO FINISH THE
VERSE. (EG: K=24)

"A _ _ _ _ GIVES _ _ _ _
   16 31 31 25   16 37 25 25

_ _ _ _ TO HIS _ _ _ _ _ ,
41 15 27 36   11 27 17 15 34

BUT A _ _ _ _ _ _ _
       42 22 35 15   26 11 27

KEEPS _ _ _ _ _ _ _ _
      21 22 26 35 15 25 16

UNDER _ _ _ _ _ _ _ . "
      13 31 27 36 34 31 25

PROVERBS 29:11

219

FILL *in the* BLANKS

COMPASSION

SHOWING COMPASSION ISN'T JUST THE RIGHT THING TO DO...IT FEELS REAL GOOD TOO!

USING THE WORDS BELOW, COMPLETE THE VERSES ON THE NEXT PAGE.

COMPASSION
FORGAVE
GRIEVANCES
ANOTHER
HAVE
CLOTHE
HOLY
LORD

HUMILITY
CHOSEN
FORGIVE
GENTLENESS
BEAR
LOVED

"THEREFORE, AS GOD'S _____

PEOPLE, _____ AND DEARLY _____,

_____ YOURSELVES WITH

_____, KINDNESS,

_____, _____ AND

PATIENCE. _____WITH EACH OTHER

AND _____ WHATEVER

_____ YOU MAY _____

AGAINST ONE _____. FORGIVE

AS THE _____ _____ YOU."

COLOSSIANS 3:12-13

SCRAMBLED VERSES

COMPASSION MEANS ACTION!
UNSCRAMBLE THE VERSES BELOW AND
COMPLETE THE NEXT PAGE TO FIND SOME
WAYS TO SHOW COMPASSION.

"ESBLS OESHT HOW CSPEEERTU YUO;
LBSES NDA OD TNO RCSEU. EOEIRCJ
IHWT HEOTS OWH JROIEEC; UMNOR
THWI SOTHE OHW NRMUO. IVEL NI
HYRNAOM HWIT NOE OAERNHT. OD
OTN EB DORPU, UBT EB GLLIWIN OT
TCSAOSEAI WHTI EOEPPL FO WLO
TIIPSOON. OD TON EB CCTEINEOD."

222

ROMANS 12:14-16

WORD SEARCH

COMPASSION MEANS BEING CONCERNED FOR OTHERS.

FIND THE WORDS UNDERLINED BELOW IN THE WORD SEARCH ON THE NEXT PAGE.

"DO NOTHING OUT OF <u>SELFISH</u> <u>AMBITION</u> OR VAIN <u>CONCEIT</u>, BUT IN <u>HUMILITY</u> CONSIDER OTHERS <u>BETTER</u> THAN YOURSELVES. EACH OF YOU <u>SHOULD</u> <u>LOOK</u> NOT ONLY TO YOUR OWN <u>INTERESTS</u>, BUT ALSO TO THE INTERESTS OF <u>OTHERS</u>."

PHILIPPIANS 2:3–4

```
K M W I B B C T I N B O
F B Y D B A Q N N Q S L
T C O N C E I T T U H W
O T H E R S T D E K O B
K K C P D V D T R E U L
H R Q O Y C L G E W L R
F J G O N T B X S R D D
G S J V B K F L T R T A
S D B E O L E S S I S M
P E T O R B V D H P T B
T P L H U M I L I T Y I
R Z T F B B D M S D N T
W A C T I N E S B F I I
H A P P B S D Z C H L O
Q L R V B P H K T K N N
```

FINISH *the* VERSE

USE THE CODE CHART BELOW TO FINISH THE
VERSES. (EG: K=24)

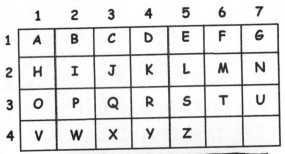

	1	2	3	4	5	6	7
1	A	B	C	D	E	F	G
2	H	I	J	K	L	M	N
3	O	P	Q	R	S	T	U
4	V	W	X	Y	Z		

"___ ___ ___ ___ ___ ___ ___ ___, IF
 12 34 31 36 21 15 34 35

___ ___ ___ ___ ___ ___ ___ IS
 35 31 26 15 31 27 15

IN A ___ ___ ___, YOU
13 11 37 17 21 36   35 22 27

WHO ARE ___ ___ ___ ___ ___ ___ ___ ___
        35 32 22 34 22 36 37 11 25

___ ___ ___ ___ ___ ___ ___ ___ ___ ___ ___ ___
 35 21 31 37 25 14 34 15 35 36 31 34 15

HIM ___ ___ ___ ___ ___ ___. BUT
    17 15 27 36 25 44

___ ___ ___ ___ ___ YOURSELF, OR YOU
 42 11 36 13 21

___ ___ ___ ___ MAY BE ___ ___ ___ ___ ___ ___.
 11 25 35 31   36 15 26 32 36 15 14

___ ___ ___ ___ ___ ___ ___ ___ ___ OTHER'S
 13 11 34 34 44   15 11 13 21

___ ___ ___ ___ ___ ___ ___, AND IN ___ ___ ___ ___
 12 37 34 14 15 27 35   36 21 22 35

WAY YOU WILL ___ ___ ___ ___ ___ ___ ___
             16 37 25 16 22 25 25

THE ___ ___ ___ OF ___ ___ ___ ___ ___ ___."
    25 11 42   13 21 34 22 35 36

GALATIANS 6:1-2

DOUBLE *the* FUN

UNSCRAMBLE THE UNDERLINED WORDS IN EACH VERSE. ON THE NEXT PAGE, PLACE YOUR ANSWERS IN THE SPACES PROVIDED AND THEN COMPLETE THE CROSSWORD PUZZLE.

1. "HAVE <u>ECMYR</u> ON ME, O GOD, ACCORDING TO YOUR UNFAILING <u>OELV</u>; ACCORDING TO YOUR GREAT COMPASSION BLOT OUT MY TRANSGRESSIONS."

   PSALM 51:1

2. "THE LORD IS <u>UCGRISAO</u> AND <u>GESOIHUTR</u>; OUR GOD IS FULL OF COMPASSION."

   PSALM 116:5

3. "THE <u>DOLR</u> IS GOOD TO ALL; HE HAS <u>OSOIPMCSAN</u> ON ALL HE HAS MADE."

   PSALM 145:9

1. _ _ _ _ _ _   _ _ _ _

2. _ _ _ _ _ _ _ _ _ _

   _ _ _ _ _ _ _ _ _ _ _

3. _ _ _ _

   _ _ _ _ _ _ _ _ _ _ _ _

229

SECRET CODES

LOVE ONE ANOTHER

TO SOLVE THE CODED VERSES BELOW, LOOK AT EACH LETTER AND WRITE THE ONE THAT COMES BEFORE IT IN THE ALPHABET.

"BCPWF BMM, MPWF FBDI PUIFS EFFQMZ, CFDBVTF MPWF DPWFST PWFS B NVMUJUVEF PG TJOT. PGGFS IPTQJUBMJUZ UP POF BOPUIFS XJUIPVU HSVNCMJOH."

230

A B C D E F G H I J K L M N O P Q R S T
U V W X Y Z

1 PETER 4:8-9

FILL *in the* BLANKS

A SPECIAL PROMISE

SOMETIMES, IT CAN BE HARD TO BE COMPAS-
SIONATE, BUT DOING SO WILL HELP YOU TO
DO THE RIGHT THING IN EVERY SITUATION.

USING THE WORDS BELOW, COMPLETE THE
VERSES ON THE NEXT PAGE.

INSULT
SYMPATHETIC
LIVE
EVIL
BROTHERS
HARMONY
INHERIT

FINALLY
BLESSING
HUMBLE
CALLED
COMPASSIONATE
REPAY
BLESSING

"_____, ALL OF YOU, _____

IN _____ WITH ONE

ANOTHER; BE _____, LOVE

AS _____, BE _____

AND _____. DO NOT _____

EVIL WITH _____ OR INSULT WITH

_____, BUT WITH _____,

BECAUSE TO THIS YOU WERE _____

SO THAT YOU MAY _____ A

_____."

1 PETER 3:8-9

FINISH *the* VERSE

HATRED

HAVE YOU EVER BEEN TOLD THAT IT'S WRONG TO HATE? BUT...SOMETIMES, YOU DO FEEL IT.

COULD THERE EVER BE A TIME THAT IT IS OKAY TO HATE? IS THERE ANYTHING THAT GOD HATES? LET'S FIND OUT!

USE THE CODE CHART BELOW TO FINISH THE VERSES. (EG: K=24)

	1	2	3	4	5	6	7
1	A	B	C	D	E	F	G
2	H	I	J	K	L	M	N
3	O	P	Q	R	S	T	U
4	V	W	X	Y	Z		

"THERE ARE ___ ___ ___ THINGS THE
        35 22 43
___ ___ ___ ___   ___ ___ ___ ___ ___,
25 31 34 14   21 11 36 15 35
___ ___ ___ ___ ___   THAT   ARE
35 15 41 15 27
                                          TO
___ ___ ___ ___ ___ ___ ___ ___ ___ ___
14 15 36 15 35 36   11 12 25 15
HIM: HAUGHTY ___ ___ ___ ___, A
              15 44 15 35
___ ___ ___ ___ ___ TONGUE, ___ ___ ___ ___ ___
25 44 22 27 17   21 11 27 14 35
THAT SHED ___ ___ ___ ___ ___ ___ ___
          22 27 27 31 13 15 27 36
BLOOD, A   HEART   THAT
                            WICKED
___ ___ ___ ___ ___ ___ ___
14 15 41 22 35 15 35
___ ___ ___ ___ ___ ___ ___, ___ ___ ___ ___
35 13 21 15 26 15 35   16 15 15 36
THAT ARE ___ ___ ___ ___ ___ TO RUSH
         33 37 22 13 24
INTO ___ ___ ___ ___, A FALSE WITNESS
     15 41 22 25
WHO ___ ___ ___ ___ ___ OUT LIES AND A
    32 31 37 34 35
___ ___ ___ WHO STIRS UP ___ ___ ___-
26 11 27   14 22 35
                                     AMONG
___ ___ ___ ___ ___ ___ ___
35 15 27 35 22 31 27
                          ___."
___ ___ ___ ___ ___ ___ ___
12 34 31 36 21 15 34 35

PROVERBS 6:16-19

235

SCRAMBLED VERSES

WHAT DOES GOD SAY?

IF IT'S OKAY FOR GOD TO HATE CERTAIN THINGS, IS THERE EVER A TIME THAT IT'S ALL RIGHT FOR ME TO HATE SOMETHING?

UNSCRAMBLE THE VERSES BELOW AND COMPLETE THE NEXT PAGE.

"UYO ERA TNO A DGO OHW STKAE EPRLUEAS NI VIEL; HTWI UOY HET DWCKIE TNNAOC DLWLE. ETH TRRONGAA TNCONA DSTAN NI RYOU ECPRNESE; UYO ETHA LAL WOH OD GNWOR."

236

PSALM 5:4-5

SCRAMBLED VERSES

A TIME FOR EVERYTHING

LET'S DIG DEEPER AND FIND OUT FROM GOD'S WORD WHEN THERE MAY BE A TIME TO HATE.

LOOK UP THE VERSES BELOW AND PUT THE WORDS IN THEIR PROPER ORDER.

IN ECCLESIASTES 3:1, IT SAYS:

EVERYTHING,   TIME   HEAVEN." "THERE A UNDER IS ACTIVITY FOR EVERY A FOR SEASON AND

AND IN VERSE 3:8, IT SAYS:

TIME "A LOVE TIME HATE." TO AND A TO

238

"
_____ _____ ____ _____

_____ _____,

_____ ___ _____ ____

_____ _____

_____ _____."

ECCLESIASTES 3:1

"
__ _____ ____ _____

_____ ____ _____ ____

_____."

ECCLESIASTES 3:8

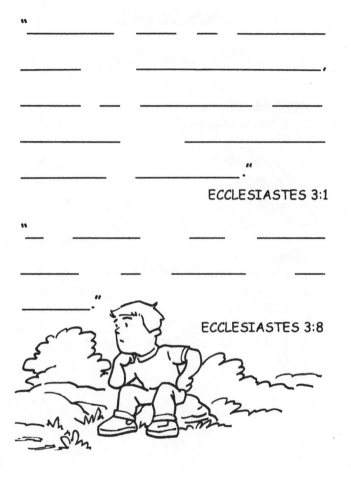

CROSSWORD

DIG, DIG, DIG!

ACROSS

1. "I GAIN UNDERSTANDING FROM YOUR
   _____."

2. "THEREFORE I _____ EVERY WRONG
   PATH."   PSALM 119:104

3. "I HATE _____-MINDED MEN."

4. "BUT I _____ YOUR LAW."
                                   PSALM 119:113

DOWN

1. "YOU ARE MY REFUGE AND MY _____."

2. "I HAVE PUT MY _____ IN YOUR
   WORD."

3. "AWAY FROM ME, YOU EVIL-_____."

4. "THAT I MAY KEEP THE COMMANDS OF
   MY _____."
                                   PSALM 119:114-115

240

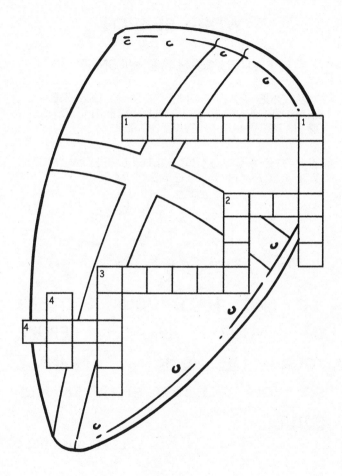

WORD SEARCH

WHEN IS HATE WRONG?

SOMEONE HAS DONE SOMETHING REALLY MEAN OR AWFUL. DO YOU HATE THE PERSON OR HATE WHAT THEY'VE DONE?

FIND THE WORDS UNDERLINED BELOW IN THE WORD SEARCH ON THE NEXT PAGE.

"DO NOT HATE YOUR BROTHER IN YOUR HEART. REBUKE YOUR NEIGHBOR FRANKLY SO YOU WILL NOT SHARE IN HIS GUILT."

LEVITICUS 19:17

```
E W D P L S K F M D P B
F H J R O N L Q S K T L
Z K L J R E B U K E D R
K M Y G F I J I K B F D
F B T H T G L D R C H X
T R H D P H B N N T K M
B T A N V B R O T H E R
K K Q N B O B D L Q S I
H R G P K R N T R D N G
E H J Z C L S G F K I U
T S E J R D Y K S P E I
A D T A D S C L T R N L
H C L T R V Q S A R O T
T P T C N T I H H R L Z
R Z C V B T S L G I W J
```

FILL *in the* BLANKS

GOD'S WORD IS CLEAR!

IT'S OKAY TO SOMETIMES HATE CERTAIN THINGS THAT OTHERS MAY DO, BUT IT IS WRONG TO HATE THE PERSON.

USING THE WORDS BELOW, COMPLETE THE VERSES ON THE NEXT PAGE.

TELL
CURSE
PRAY
LOVE
MISTREAT
HATE
GOOD
ENEMIES
BLESS
HEAR

244

"BUT I _____ YOU WHO _____

ME: _____ YOUR _____,

DO _____ TO THOSE WHO _____

YOU, _____ THOSE WHO _____

YOU, _____ FOR THOSE WHO

_____ YOU."

LUKE 6:27–28

245

FINISH the VERSE

L♡VE
A FEELING...OR AN ACTION?

IF LOVE IS JUST A FEELING, WHAT HAPPENS WHEN WE GET ANGRY WITH SOMEONE? DO WE NO LONGER LOVE THEM?

WHAT IF OUR PARENTS WANT US TO DO SOME-THING WE JUST DON'T WANT TO DO; WE COULD BE REALLY ANGRY AT THEM. BECAUSE WE DON'T HAVE LOVING FEELINGS RIGHT AT THAT MOMENT, DOES THAT MEAN WE NO LONGER LOVE THEM?

USE THE CODE CHART BELOW TO FINISH THE VERSE. (EG: K=24)

	1	2	3	4	5	6	7
1	A	B	C	D	E	F	G
2	H	I	J	K	L	M	N
3	O	P	Q	R	S	T	U
4	V	W	X	Y	Z		

HOW DOES GOD LOVE US?

"FOR $\underset{17\ \ 31\ \ 14}{\rule{1.5cm}{0.4pt}}$ SO $\underset{25\ \ 31\ \ 41\ \ 15\ \ 14}{\rule{2.5cm}{0.4pt}}$

THE $\underset{42\ \ 31\ \ 34\ \ 25\ \ 14}{\rule{2.5cm}{0.4pt}}$ THAT HE

$\underset{17\ \ 11\ \ 41\ \ 15}{\rule{2cm}{0.4pt}}$ $\underset{21\ \ 22\ \ 35}{\rule{1.5cm}{0.4pt}}$ $\underset{31\ \ 27\ \ 15}{\rule{1.5cm}{0.4pt}}$

AND $\underset{31\ \ 27\ \ 25\ \ 44}{\rule{2cm}{0.4pt}}$ $\underset{35\ \ 31\ \ 27}{\rule{1.5cm}{0.4pt}}$, THAT

$\underset{42\ \ 21\ \ 31\ \ 15\ \ 41\ \ 15\ \ 34}{\rule{3.5cm}{0.4pt}}$ BELIEVES $\underset{22\ \ 27}{\rule{1cm}{0.4pt}}$

$\underset{21\ \ 22\ \ 26}{\rule{1.5cm}{0.4pt}}$ $\underset{35\ \ 21\ \ 11\ \ 25\ \ 25}{\rule{2.5cm}{0.4pt}}$ NOT

$\underset{32\ \ 15\ \ 34\ \ 22\ \ 35\ \ 21}{\rule{3cm}{0.4pt}}$ BUT HAVE

$\underset{15\ \ 36\ \ 15\ \ 34\ \ 27\ \ 11\ \ 25}{\rule{3.5cm}{0.4pt}}$ $\underset{25\ \ 22\ \ 16\ \ 15}{\rule{2cm}{0.4pt}}$."

JOHN 3:16

MAYBE, IF WE CHOOSE TO TREAT OTHERS KINDLY,
NO MATTER WHAT, OR WE DO AS ASKED, OUR *ACT*
OF OBEDIENCE DEMONSTRATES OUR LOVE!

247

COLOR *the* PICTURE

LOVE IN ACTION!

IN 1 JOHN 3:16 AND 18 THE APOSTLE JOHN TELLS US OF THE KIND OF LOVE THAT GOD HAS FOR US AND HOW WE SHOULD ACT BECAUSE OF THAT LOVE.

"THIS IS HOW WE KNOW WHAT LOVE IS: JESUS CHRIST LAID DOWN HIS LIFE FOR US."

and:

"DEAR CHILDREN, LET US NOT LOVE WITH WORDS OR TONGUE BUT WITH ACTIONS AND IN TRUTH."

SECRET CODES

LOVE ONE ANOTHER.

TO SOLVE THE CODED VERSES BELOW, LOOK AT EACH LETTER AND WRITE THE ONE THAT COMES BEFORE IT IN THE ALPHABET.

"B OFX DPNNBOE J HJWF ZPV: MPWF POF BOPUIFS. BT J IBWF MPWFE ZPV, TP ZPV NVTU MPWF POF BOPUIFS. CZ UIJT BMM NFO XJMM LOPX UIBU ZPV BSF NZ EJTDJQMFT, JG ZPV MPWF POF BOPUIFS."

ABCDEFGHIJKLMNOPQRST
UVWXYZ

JOHN 13:34-35

251

MULTIPLE CHOICE

"YOU HAVE HEARD THAT IT WAS SAID, 'LOVE YOUR NEIGHBOR AND HATE YOUR ENEMY.' BUT I TELL YOU: LOVE YOUR ENEMIES AND PRAY FOR THOSE WHO PERSECUTE YOU."

MATTHEW 5:43-44

BASED ON THE VERSES ABOVE, WHAT SHOULD BE DONE IN THE FOLLOWING SITUATIONS?

1. A GIRL AT SCHOOL HAS BEEN SPREADING LIES ABOUT YOU.
   A) CHALLENGE HER TO A FIGHT.
   B) INVITE HER TO YOUR HOUSE AND GET TO KNOW HER.
   C) REPORT HER TO THE PRINCIPAL.

2. SOMEONE STOLE YOUR BIKE AND YOU KNOW WHO IT IS.
   A) PHONE THE POLICE.
   B) ASK FOR IT BACK AND OFFER YOUR OLD BIKE FOR FREE.
   C) YOU AND YOUR BUDDIES SHOULD GO AND CONFRONT HIM.

3. SOMEONE YOU THOUGHT WAS YOUR
   FRIEND COPIED YOUR BOOK REPORT AND
   HAS BLAMED YOU FOR CHEATING.
   - A) GOD REVEALS THE TRUTH AND YOU
     DECIDE YOU CAN NO LONGER BE
     FRIENDS.
   - B) YOU TAKE THE BLAME.
   - C) GOD REVEALS THE TRUTH AND YOU
     OFFER FORGIVENESS.

4. KIDS AT SCHOOL LAUGH AT YOU BECAUSE
   OF YOUR FAITH.
   - A) IN THE FUTURE, YOU DECIDE TO
     KEEP YOUR FAITH A SECRET.
   - B) YOU DECIDE TO USE THIS AS AN
     OPPORTUNITY TO SHARE YOUR
     FAITH.
   - C) BOLDLY CONFRONT THEM AND
     CONDEMN THEM FOR THEIR SIN.

5. JESUS WAS UNFAIRLY JUDGED AND SENT
   TO THE CROSS.
   - A) HE ASKED HIS FATHER TO FORGIVE
     THOSE RESPONSIBLE, THEN DIED
     FOR US ALL.
   - B) HE CALLED UPON LEGIONS OF
     ANGELS TO SAVE HIM.
   - C) HE CRIED OUT FOR MERCY.

DOUBLE *the* FUN

UNSCRAMBLE THE UNDERLINED WORDS IN
EACH VERSE. ON THE NEXT PAGE, PLACE YOUR
ANSWERS IN THE SPACES PROVIDED AND
THEN COMPLETE THE CROSSWORD PUZZLE.

1. "I LOVE YOU, O LORD, MY RGSTTHNE."

     PSALM 18:1

2. "SURELY ODSOGESN AND VEOL WILL FOL-
   LOW ME ALL THE DAYS OF MY FLEI, AND
   I WILL ELWDL IN THE OHESU OF THE
   LORD FOREVER."

     PSALM 23:6

3. "MAY YOUR UNFAILING LOVE TRSE UPON
   US, O LORD, EVEN AS WE PUT OUR OPHE
   IN YOU."

     PSALM 33:22

254

1. __ __ __ __ __ __ __ __

2. __ __ __ __ __ __ __ __ __ __ __

__ __ __ __ __ __ __ __ __

__ __ __ __ __

3. __ __ __ __ __ __ __ __

255

SCRAMBLED VERSES

WHAT DOES GOD SAY?

WHEN WE BEGIN TO UNDERSTAND JUST HOW MUCH GOD LOVES US, AND HOW MUCH WE DON'T DESERVE IT, WE REALIZE THE DEPTH OF HIS MERCY AND GRACE.

THIS CAN HELP US TO SEE OTHERS DIFFERENTLY AND HOPEFULLY OFFER THEM GRACE AS WELL IF THEY DO THINGS THAT HURT US.

UNSCRAMBLE THE VERSE BELOW AND COMPLETE THE NEXT PAGE.

"TBU VLEO URYO MEEIENS, OD ODGO OT ETMH, NDA NLDE OT MEHT TTUIWHO PICXEETGN OT TGE HAYNTGIN CAKB. TNEH UORY WREADR LILW EB TGERA, DAN OYU IWLL EB ONSS FO HET OTSM GIHH, SBCEEUA EH SI DKNI OT TEH TGUULERFAN DNA WDKEIC."

LUKE 6:35

257

CROSSWORD

A FRAGRANT OFFERING

ACROSS

1. " BE _____ OF GOD, THEREFORE."
2. "AS DEARLY LOVED _____."
3. "_____ LIVE A LIFE OF LOVE."
4. "JUST AS _____ LOVED US."

DOWN

1. "AND GAVE _____ UP FOR US."
2. "AS A _____ OFFERING."
3. "AND _____ TO GOD."

EPHESIANS 5:1-2

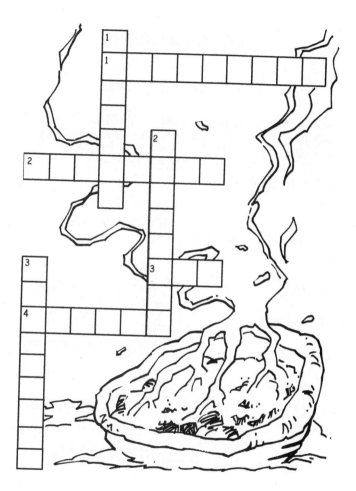

259

WORD SEARCH

LOVE COVERS IT ALL!

WE DO THINGS THAT ARE WRONG...OTHERS
DO THINGS THAT ARE WRONG AND HURTFUL.
WE WOULD WANT OTHERS TO RESPOND WITH
LOVE AND FORGIVE US; PERHAPS WE SHOULD
DO THE SAME?

FIND THE SINS, LISTED BELOW, IN THE WORD
SEARCH ON THE NEXT PAGE.

ANGER

JEALOUSY

GOSSIP

SLANDER

LYING

ENVY

STEALING

HATRED

THEFT

CHEATING

```
T H J G F G L D R D K R
F E N V Y H B N E H S G
A M Y D P J R R T Q N C
K N T N V E T D L D P F
F R G N B A N T R K T L
T T Q E H L S G F P H T
B K G Z R O Y K S R E Z
K R J J R U C L T R F J
H H T A D S Q S D R T R
M S L T L Y I N G I B E
C H E A T I N G O P L D
H C C V B K F M S T R N
T P P L S L Q S S D D A
S T E A L I N G I F X L
W D J R B J I K P H M S
```

MULTIPLE CHOICE

"DO TO OTHERS AS YOU WOULD HAVE THEM
DO TO YOU."

LUKE 6:31

AFTER READING THE VERSE ABOVE, WHAT WOULD
BE THE RIGHT CHOICES BELOW?

1. PETER BETRAYED JESUS THE NIGHT OF HIS
   TRIAL.
   - A) JESUS FOREVER BANNED HIM FROM
     HEAVEN.
   - B) JESUS EXPECTED PETER TO MAKE IT
     UP TO HIM.
   - C) JESUS FORGAVE HIM.
2. JESUS TOLD OF A MAN WHO WAS FORGIVEN
   HIS DEBTS.
   - A) THE MAN WAS NOW FREE TO COLLECT
     FROM THOSE WHO OWED HIM.
   - B) HE SHOULD FORGIVE OTHERS THEIR
     DEBTS TO HIM.
   - C) HE SHOULD PAY IT BACK ANYWAY.
3. BOTH YOU AND YOUR FRIEND HAVE BEEN
   OFFERED THE SAME ROLE IN THE SCHOOL
   PLAY.
   - A) DO YOUR BEST AT THE AUDITION.
   - B) OFFER A BRIBE TO GET THE PART.
   - C) DECLINE THE PART.

4. JESUS TOLD OF A FATHER WHO WAITED FOR A REBELLIOUS SON TO RETURN HOME.
    A) THE FATHER SHOULD WELCOME HIM BACK AND CELEBRATE.
    B) HE SHOULD NOT ALLOW THE SON BACK UNTIL HE PAYS BACK THE MONEY HE SQUANDERED.
    C) HE SHOULD TAKE HIM BACK BUT TREAT HIM AS ONE OF HIS SERVANTS.

5. AN INJURED MAN LIES ON THE SIDE OF THE ROAD.
    A) PASS BY, HOPING SOMEONE ELSE WILL TAKE CARE OF HIM.
    B) MAKE HIM COMFORTABLE, THEN RUN FOR HELP.
    C) CHECK HIS CLOTHING FOR ANY VALUABLES.

6. YOUR PARENTS HAVE ASKED A FAVOR, THAT YOU WOULD CLEAN THE CARS.
    A) YOU AGREE BUT DECIDE LATER NOT TO BOTHER.
    B) YOU WILL...AS LONG AS THEY PAY YOU.
    C) YOU DO IT WILLINGLY, REALIZING HOW MUCH THEY DO FOR YOU.

FINISH *the* VERSE

USE THE CODE CHART BELOW TO FINISH THE
VERSES. (EG: K=24)

	1	2	3	4	5	6	7
1	A	B	C	D	E	F	G
2	H	I	J	K	L	M	N
3	O	P	Q	R	S	T	U
4	V	W	X	Y	Z		

"IF YOU ___ ___ ___ ___ THOSE WHO
     25 31 41 15

___ ___ ___ ___ YOU, WHAT ___ ___ ___ ___ ___ ___
25 31 41 15   13 34 15 14 22 36

IS ___ ___ ___ ___ TO YOU? EVEN
    36 21 11 36

' ___ ___ ___ ___ ___ ___ ___ '   ___ ___ ___ ___
 35 22 27 27 15 34 35   25 31 41 15

___ ___ ___ ___ ___ WHO   ___ ___ ___ ___
36 21 31 35 15   25 31 41 15

THEM. AND IF YOU DO ___ ___ ___ ___ TO
                       17 31 31 14

___ ___ ___ ___ ___ WHO ARE ___ ___ ___ ___
36 21 31 35 15   17 31 31 14

TO YOU, WHAT ___ ___ ___ ___ ___ ___ IS
             13 34 15 14 22 36

THAT TO ___ ___ ___ ? EVEN
          44 31 37

' ___ ___ ___ ___ ___ ___ ___ ' DO THAT.
 35 22 27 27 15 34 35

LUKE 6:32-33

265

SCRAMBLED VERSES

GOD'S WAY IS CERTAINLY DIFFERENT!

THE WORLD WOULD LEAD YOU TO BELIEVE THAT YOU SHOULD PUT YOURSELF ABOVE ALL OTHERS. BUT YOU'VE LEARNED HOW GOD WANTS YOU TO THINK, THAT THERE IS GREAT BLESSING IN PUTTING OTHERS BEFORE YOURSELF.

TRY IT HIS WAY!

LOOK UP THE VERSES BELOW AND PUT THE WORDS IN THEIR PROPER ORDER.

IN PROVERBS 24:17, IT SAYS:

ENEMY GLOAT WHEN NOT REJOICE," YOUR STUMBLES, "DO HEART FALLS; YOUR NOT LET HE DO WHEN

AND IN ROMANS 12:14, IT SAYS:

YOU; THOSE CURSE." PERSECUTE "BLESS NOT WHO AND BLESS DO

CROSSWORD

FEAR WORRY

FEAR AND WORRY! THESE TWO ARE REAL FAITH-BUSTERS AND ARE GUARANTEED TO KNOCK YOU RIGHT OFF YOUR FEET.

BUT, *HOW* CAN YOU OVERCOME THEM? LET'S CONTINUE ON AND YOU'LL SEE HOW OVER THE NEXT FEW PAGES.

ACROSS
1. "THE LORD IS MY _____ AND MY SALVATION."
2. "WHOM SHALL I _____?"
3. "THE LORD IS THE _____ OF MY LIFE."
4. "OF WHOM SHALL I BE _____?"
   PSALM 27:1

DOWN
1. "THOUGH AN ARMY _____ ME."
2. "MY HEART WILL NOT _____,"
3. "THOUGH WAR BREAK _____ AGAINST ME."
4. "EVEN THEN WILL I BE _____."
   PSALM 27:3

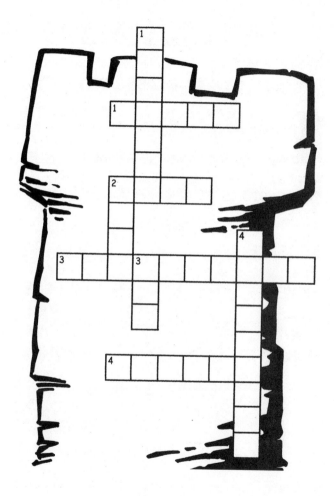

269

FILL *in the* BLANKS

DON'T WORRY *and* BE CONTENT!

USING THE WORDS BELOW, COMPLETE THE VERSE ON THE NEXT PAGE.

FEAR AND WORRY CAN BE PRODUCED WHEN WE PUT TOO MUCH TRUST IN MONEY OR POSSESSIONS. SO BE CAREFUL.

FORSAKE
GOD
NEVER
HAVE
YOU
CONTENT

LIVES
LEAVE
FREE
WILL
LOVE
MONEY

"KEEP YOUR _____ _____
FROM THE _____ OF _____
AND BE _____ WITH
WHAT YOU _____, BECAUSE
_____ HAS SAID, '_____ WILL
I _____ _____; NEVER _____
I _____ YOU.'"

HEBREWS 13:5

271

SECRET CODES

PUT YOUR TRUST IN THE LORD

TO SOLVE THE CODED VERSES BELOW, LOOK
AT EACH LETTER AND WRITE THE ONE THAT
COMES BEFORE IT IN THE ALPHABET.

"DBTU ZPVS DBSFT PO UIF MPSE BOE
IF XJMM TVTUBJO ZPV; IF XJMM
OFWFS MFU UIF SJHIUFPVT GBMM."
PSALM 55:22

"CVU ZPV, P HPE, XJMM CSJOH EPXO
UIF XJDLFE JOUP UIF QJU PG
DPSSVQUJPO; CMPPEUIJSTUZ BOE
EFDFJUGVM NFO XJMM OPU MJWF
PVU IBMG UIFJS EBZT. CVU BT GPS
NF, J USVTU JO ZPV."
PSALM 55:23

A B C D E F G H I J K L M N O P Q R S T
U V W X Y Z

"_____ _____ _____
__ ___ _____ ___
__ _____ _____
__ __ __; __ __ ___ _
___ ____ ___ ___
_____ _____."

"____ ____, __ ____,
_____ _____ _____
____ _____ ____
___ ___ __ ___-
_____; _____-
_____ ____ ___
_____ ___ ___
___ ____ ___ ____
__ ___. ____ ___ ____
__ __, __ _____ __
__ __."

DOUBLE *the* FUN

UNSCRAMBLE THE UNDERLINED WORDS IN EACH VERSE. ON THE NEXT PAGE, PLACE YOUR ANSWERS IN THE SPACES PROVIDED AND THEN COMPLETE THE CROSSWORD PUZZLE.

1. "THE <u>ARFE</u> OF THE LORD IS <u>UPER</u>, ENDURING <u>RREEFVO</u>. THE <u>AEONNRICSD</u> OF THE LORD ARE SURE AND ALTOGETHER RIGHTEOUS."

PSALM 19:9

2. "EVEN THOUGH I <u>KAWL</u> THROUGH THE <u>YALVLE</u> OF THE <u>HAWSOD</u> OF DEATH, I WILL FEAR NO <u>LEIV</u>, FOR YOU ARE WITH ME; YOUR <u>DRO</u> AND YOUR STAFF, THEY <u>OFMTCOR</u> ME."

PSALM 23:4

1. ___ ___ ___ ___   ___ ___ ___ ___
   ___ ___ ___ ___ ___ ___ ___
   ___ ___ ___ ___ ___ ___ ___ ___ ___ ___
2. ___ ___ ___ ___ ___ ___   ___ ___ ___ ___
   ___ ___ ___ ___ ___ ___   ___ ___ ___ ___
   ___ ___ ___   ___ ___ ___ ___ ___ ___ ___

275

SCRAMBLED VERSES

HOW VALUABLE ARE YOU?

TO FIND OUT, LOOK UP THE VERSES BELOW AND PUT THE WORDS IN THEIR PROPER ORDER.

IN MATTHEW 6:25-26, IT SAYS:

WORRY YOU IMPORTANT "THEREFORE NOT FOOD, MORE WHAT IMPORTANT I YOU, CLOTHES?" DRINK; ABOUT BODY EAT MORE THE LIFE, YOUR TELL WILL WHAT DO YOUR WEAR. BODY, YOU LIFE AND ABOUT OR THAN IS WILL OR THAN NOT

BIRDS FATHER MUCH THEM. HEAVENLY DO VALUABLE "LOOK THAN AIR; REAP STORE MORE SOW BARNS, AWAY AT THE YOUR OF FEEDS NOT OR NOT THEY OR IN THE THEY?" AND YOU YET ARE

" Therefore _____ _____ __ _____

_____ , _____ __ _____ _____

_____ _____ __ _____ _____ ,

__ Drink ; __ _____ __

_____ _____ , _____ __

_____ _____ Wear .

_____ _____ __ _____

_____ , __ _____ _____

_____ _____ Clotes ?"

" Look _____ __ _____

_____ __ Air ; _____ __

_____ __ __ _____ _____

_____ _____ __ Barns ,

_____ _____ __ Them .

_____ __ __ _____ _____

_____ _____ __ _____

They ?"

FINISH *the* VERSE

USE THE CODE CHART BELOW TO FINISH THE
VERSES. (EG: K=24)

	1	2	3	4	5	6	7
1	A	B	C	D	E	F	G
2	H	I	J	K	L	M	N
3	O	P	Q	R	S	T	U
4	V	W	X	Y	Z		

"__ __ __ OF __ __ __ BY
  42 21 31   44 31 37

__ __ __ __ __ __ __ __ CAN ADD A
42 31 34 34 44 22 27 17

                                TO
__ __ __ __ __ __   __ __ __ __
35 22 27 17 25 15   21 31 37 34

HIS __ __ __ __? AND __ __ __ DO
       25 22 16 15   42 21 44

YOU   WORRY
                   __ __ __ __ __
                   11 12 31 37 36

__ __ __ __ __ __ __? SEE HOW THE
13 25 31 36 21 15 35

__ __ __ __ __ __ OF THE
25 22 25 22 15 35

__ __ __ __ __ __ __ __ __. THEY
16 22 15 25 14   17 34 31 42

DO NOT   __ __ __ __ __ OR
            25 11 12 31 34

__ __ __ __."
35 32 22 27

MATTHEW 6:27–28

WORD SEARCH

FIND THE WORDS UNDERLINED BELOW IN THE WORD SEARCH ON THE NEXT PAGE.

"YET I <u>TELL</u> YOU THAT NOT EVEN <u>SOLOMON</u> IN ALL HIS <u>SPLENDOR</u> WAS <u>DRESSED</u> LIKE ONE OF THESE. IF THAT IS HOW GOD <u>CLOTHES</u> THE <u>GRASS</u> OF THE <u>FIELD</u>, WHICH IS HERE <u>TODAY</u> AND <u>TOMORROW</u> IS <u>THROWN</u> INTO THE <u>FIRE</u>, WILL HE NOT MUCH MORE <u>CLOTHE</u> YOU, O YOU OF LITTLE <u>FAITH</u>?"

MATTHEW 6:29-30

```
F H T D F Q B F K D D L
C L O T H E S Q K T F V
D R D N P G L T E E T K
E T A P V F B R N L O Q
S A Y Z X B I H T L M X
S R I J B F B E C Q O M
E H T T K R M T L D R C
R S O L O M O N L D R L
D D P G R D N K R P O G
N C Z L D S S L F R W B
B W P C E S Y F S B N H
H Z O V A N C H A R X L
T D J R B T D L Z I L T
R J G Z H K D O H P T Z
W T C L O T H E R T B H
```

SECRET CODES

SO...DON'T WORRY!

TO SOLVE THE CODED VERSES BELOW, LOOK AT EACH LETTER AND WRITE THE ONE THAT COMES BEFORE IT IN THE ALPHABET.

"TP EP OPU XPSSZ, TBZJOH, 'XIBU TIBMM XF FBU?' PS 'ZIBU TIBMM XF ESJOL?' PS 'XIBU TIBMM XF XFBS?'"

MATTHEW 6:31

"EP OPU CF BOYJPVT BCPVU BOZUIJOH, CVU JO FWFSZUIJOH, CZ QSBZFS BOE QFUJUJPO, XJUI UIBOLTHJWJOH, QSFTFOU ZPVS SFRVFTUT UP HPE."

PHILIPPIANS 4:6

282

ABCDEFGHIJKLMNOPQRST
UVWXYZ

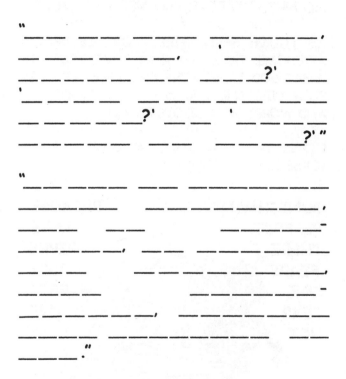

FILL *in the* BLANKS

NO NEED TO FEAR, NO NEED TO WORRY!

AS YOU'VE SEEN, GOD'S LOVE IS PRETTY AWESOME. TRUST IN THAT LOVE, TRUST IN WHAT GOD IS WILLING AND ABLE TO DO IN YOUR LIFE AND YOU WILL FIND THAT FEAR AND WORRY WILL BE OVERCOME!

USING THE WORDS BELOW, COMPLETE THE VERSE ON THE NEXT PAGE.

PUNISHMENT   BECAUSE
PERFECT   LOVE
THERE   DRIVES
FEARS   FEAR
ONE   PERFECT
FEAR   LOVE
NOT   LOVE

"_____ IS NO _____ IN

_____. BUT _____

_____ _____ OUT FEAR,

_____ _____ HAS TO

DO WITH _____.

THE _____ WHO _____ IS

_____ MADE _____ IN

_____."

1 JOHN 4:18

285

CROSSWORD

YOU'VE LEARNED ABOUT THE MOST IMPORTANT THING OF ALL...GOD'S LOVE FOR YOU. YOU'VE LEARNED HOW TO OVERCOME FEELINGS THAT CAN HARM YOU OR OTHERS AND HOW THAT INVOLVES TRUSTING GOD.

LET'S DISCOVER MORE ABOUT TRUST!

ACROSS

1. "HE WILL MAKE YOUR _____."
2. "_____ LIKE THE DAWN."
3. "THE _____ OF YOUR CAUSE."
4. "LIKE THE NOONDAY _____."

PSALM 37:6

DOWN

1. "_____ IN THE LORD."
2. "WITH ALL YOUR _____."
3. "AND _____ NOT."
4. "ON YOUR OWN _____ STANDING."

PROVERBS 3:5

287

FINISH *the* VERSE

TRUST AND REJOICE!

YOU CAN KNOW AN INCREDIBLE JOY WHEN YOU PUT YOUR TRUST IN THE LORD. BECAUSE YOU KNOW HOW MUCH HE LOVES YOU, YOU CAN BELIEVE THAT HE WILL ALWAYS WORK OUT EVERYTHING FOR THE BEST.

USE THE CODE CHART BELOW TO FINISH THE VERSE. (EG: K=24)

	1	2	3	4	5	6	7
1	A	B	C	D	E	F	G
2	H	I	J	K	L	M	N
3	O	P	Q	R	S	T	U
4	V	W	X	Y	Z		

"_____ _____ _____ _____ _____ WHO _____ _____ _____ _____
 36 21 31 35 15   24 27 31 42

YOUR _____ _____ _____ _____ WILL _____ _____ _____ _____ _____
     27 11 26 15   36 34 37 35 36

IN YOU, _____ _____ _____   _____ _____ _____, LORD,
        16 31 34   44 31 37

HAVE _____ _____ _____ _____ _____   _____ _____ _____-
     27 15 41 15 34   16 31 34

_____ _____ _____ _____ _____ THOSE _____ _____ _____
35 11 24 15 27   42 21 31

_____ _____ _____ _____ _____ _____ _____."
35 15 15 24 44 31 37

PSALM 9:10

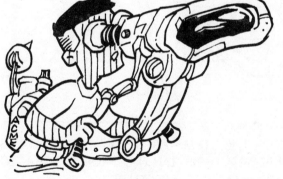

COLOR *the* PICTURE

UNFAILING LOVE

"BUT I TRUST IN YOUR UNFAILING LOVE; MY HEART REJOICES IN YOUR SALVATION."

PSALM 13:5

COPY THE ITEMS ABOVE ON THE NEXT PAGE, PLACING THEM IN THE PROPER LOCATION, THEN COLOR THE PICTURE.

SCRAMBLED VERSES

WHAT DOES GOD WANT?

NOT EVERYONE WILL BE OUR FRIEND. AT TIMES THERE WILL BE PROBLEMS WITH OTHER PEOPLE...THEY JUST MAY NOT LIKE US AND SOMETIMES IT WILL BE HARD TO UNDERSTAND WHY.

WHAT WOULD GOD WANT YOU TO DO IN A SITUATION LIKE THIS?

UNSCRAMBLE THE VERSE BELOW AND FIND OUT.

"NI UYO I SRTTU, O YM DGO. OD TNO LTE EM EB TPU OT MSHEA, RNO ETL YM MNEEESI TPHRMUI EORV EM."

"__ ___ __ _____ __,
_ __ ___. __ ___
__ __ ___ __ ___
__ _____, ___
___ __ _____
_____ ___ _
__."

PSALM 25:2

DOUBLE *the* FUN

UNSCRAMBLE THE UNDERLINED WORDS IN
EACH VERSE. ON THE NEXT PAGE, PLACE YOUR
ANSWERS IN THE SPACES PROVIDED AND
THEN COMPLETE THE CROSSWORD PUZZLE.

1. "SOME TRUST IN <u>OAITHRSC</u> AND SOME
   IN <u>RHESOS</u>, BUT WE TRUST IN THE <u>MNEA</u>
   OF THE LORD OUR GOD."

   PSALM 20:7

2. "BUT I <u>SURTT</u> IN YOU, O LORD; I SAY,
   'YOU ARE MY GOD.'"

   PSALM 31:14

3. "IN HIM OUR <u>RHESAT</u> <u>JECERIO</u>, FOR WE
   TRUST IN HIS <u>OYLH</u> NAME."

   PSALM 33:21

1. ___ ___ ___ ___ ___ ___ ___ ___ ___ ___
   ___ ___ ___ ___ ___ ___   ___ ___ ___ ___

2. ___ ___ ___ ___ ___

3. ___ ___ ___ ___ ___ ___   ___ ___ ___ ___ ___ ___
   ___ ___ ___ ___

295

SCRAMBLED VERSES

LOOK UP THE VERSES BELOW AND PUT THE WORDS IN THEIR PROPER ORDER.

TOLD HEARTS HAVE PLACE FATHER'S "DO GOING." YOU HOUSE TRUST MANY YOU, I I COME WOULD ROOMS; THAT WAY GOING TROUBLED. PREPARE GOD; YOUR MAY BE SO, A PLACE WILL BACK I YOU PREPARE AND TRUST ME. YOU YOU. TO I GO ARE WHERE KNOW THE WHERE NOT LET AND A PLACE I AM ALSO IN IN MY TAKE BE WITH AM IT WERE IN TO THE I AM. TO FOR BE ME THERE YOU. NOT IF IF FOR AND ALSO

JOHN 14:1-4

FILL *in the* BLANKS

OVERFLOWING!

BLESSINGS ARE MANY WHEN YOU CHOOSE TO TRUST IN THE LORD. BUT REALLY TRUSTING IN GOD IS ONLY POSSIBLE AS YOU ASK HIM FOR THE POWER TO DO SO.

TRY LETTING GO AND ALLOW GOD TO LEAD YOU AND WORK OUT ALL THINGS IN YOUR LIFE.

USING THE WORDS BELOW, COMPLETE THE VERSE ON THE NEXT PAGE.

OVERFLOW   GOD
HOPE   SPIRIT
PEACE   POWER
TRUST   MAY
HOLY   FILL
HIM   JOY

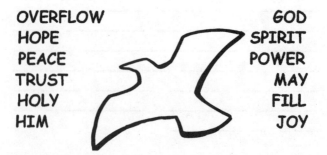

"_____ THE _____ OF _____

_____ YOU WITH ALL _____ AND

_____ AS YOU _____ IN

_____, SO THAT YOU MAY

_____ WITH HOPE BY

THE _____ OF THE _____

_____."

ROMANS 15:13

NOW, THAT'S A BLESSING!

299

SECRET CODES

JEALOUSY AND GREED

A GREAT WAY TO LOSE THE FEELING OF JOY AND PEACE IS TO LET SOMETHING LIKE JEALOUSY OR GREED GAIN A FOOTHOLD IN YOUR LIFE.

NOTHING WILL DAMPEN THE FRUIT OF THE SPIRIT AS FAST AS THESE TWO.

BUT ONCE AGAIN, THE WORD WILL GIVE US GOD'S FEELINGS ON THESE AND THE SOLUTIONS HE HAS TO OVERCOME THEM.

TO SOLVE THE CODED VERSE BELOW, LOOK AT EACH LETTER AND WRITE THE ONE THAT COMES BEFORE IT IN THE ALPHABET.

"LFFQ ZPVS MJWFT GSFF GSPN UIF MPWF PG NPOFZ BOE CF DPOUFOU XJUI XIBU ZPV IBWF, CFDBVTF HPE IBT TBJE, 'OFWFS XJMM J MFBWF ZPV; OFWFS XJMM J GPSTBLF ZPV.'"

HEBREWS 13:5

300

A B C D E F G H I J K L M N O P Q R S T
U V W X Y Z

"———— ————— ——————
—— —— —— ———— —— ——
———— —— —————— ——————
—— ———————— ————
—— —— —— ——— ————,
—— —— —— —— ——
——— ————,' —————
—— —— — —— ————
———; —————— ————
— ———————— ———.'"

301

FINISH *the* VERSE

AN EVIL R O O T

MONEY IN ITSELF IS NOT EVIL, BUT WHEN A
PERSON WANTS MORE AND MORE OF IT,
THAT'S WHEN THE TROUBLE BEGINS. WE
BEGIN TO LOOK AT WHAT OTHERS HAVE AND
START TO BELIEVE THAT WE'VE JUST GOT TO
HAVE IT TOO IF WE ARE TO BE HAPPY.

USE THE CODE CHART BELOW TO FINISH THE
VERSE. (EG: K=24)

	1	2	3	4	5	6	7
1	A	B	C	D	E	F	G
2	H	I	J	K	L	M	N
3	O	P	Q	R	S	T	U
4	V	W	X	Y	Z		

" ___ ___ ___ THE ___ ___ ___ ___ OF
  16 31 34   25 31 41 15

___ ___ ___ ___ ___ IS A ___ ___ ___ ___ OF
26 31 27 15 44   34 31 31 36

ALL ___ ___ ___ ___ ___ OF ___ ___ ___ ___.
    24 22 27 14 35   15 41 22 25

SOME ___ ___ ___ ___ ___ ___, ___ ___ ___ ___ ___
    32 15 31 32 25 15   15 11 17 15 34

FOR ___ ___ ___ ___ ___, HAVE ___ ___ ___-
   26 31 27 15 44   42 11 27

___ ___ ___ ___ ___ FROM THE ___ ___ ___ ___ ___
14 15 34 15 14   16 11 22 36 21

AND ___ ___ ___ ___ ___ ___ ___
    32 22 15 34 13 15 14

___ ___ ___ ___ ___ ___ ___ ___ ___ WITH
36 21 15 26 35 15 25 41 15 35

___ ___ ___ ___ ___ ___ ___ ___ ___ ___."
26 11 27 44   17 34 22 15 16 35

1 TIMOTHY 6:10

303

SCRAMBLED VERSES

ABUNDANCE...*or* EMPTINESS?

DO YOU THINK THAT IF YOU HAD EVERY-
THING IN THE WORLD YOU WANTED, YOU
WOULD FINALLY BE HAPPY?
OR WOULD YOU STILL FEEL EMPTY AND
UNSATISFIED?

UNSCRAMBLE THE VERSE BELOW AND FIND
OUT.

"NHET EH ASID OT TMHE, 'TAWHC
TUO! EB NO YRUO ADRUG AASTNGI
LAL NKSDI FO EERDG; A N'SAM EIFL
EDSO NTO NSCSITO NI ETH
DAUANBCEN FO SHI OSESNSIPSOS.'"

LUKE 12:15

FILL THEM IN

DEATH TO SIN!

LOOK UP COLOSSIANS 3:5 IN YOUR BIBLE.

ON THE NEXT PAGE, FILL IN THE BOXES WITH THE SINS THAT ARE DESERVING OF DEATH.

WORD SEARCH

FIND THE WORDS UNDERLINED BELOW IN THE WORD SEARCH ON THE NEXT PAGE.

"BE <u>SHEPHERDS</u> OF GOD'S <u>FLOCK</u> THAT IS IS UNDER YOUR <u>CARE</u>, <u>SERVING</u> AS <u>OVERSEERS</u>—NOT BECAUSE YOU MUST, BUT <u>BECAUSE</u> YOU ARE WILLING, AS <u>GOD</u> WANTS YOU TO BE; NOT <u>GREEDY</u> FOR <u>MONEY</u>, BUT <u>EAGER</u> TO <u>SERVE</u>."

1 PETER 5:2

JUST IN CASE YOU THINK THIS VERSE DOESN'T APPLY TO YOU, THINK AGAIN! AN OVERSEER IS JUST SOMEONE WHO LOOKS OUT FOR THE INTERESTS OF SOMEONE ELSE. MAYBE FOR YOU, IT MIGHT BE A FRIEND OR A YOUNGER BROTHER OR SISTER.

BUT, THE REAL KEY IN THIS VERSE IS BEING *EAGER TO SERVE!*

308

```
F L O C K D C L D F Q D
G M Z N H S E M D T X Q
N R O G R S A O Z B M J
I H T N D T G L B E C T
V S Z C E T E N H C L H
R D P V B Y R C Q A G M
E C J S E R V E D U B K
S D G Z H B R L D S H X
O V E R S E E R S E L W
N D C F G L P R B L T S
B J A H F M G H R W Z P
H T R P B W K S E B J H
R J E G R E E D Y R C Z
W D Z X R S S H T V D K
H K J B L Y H G D K Q S
```

CROSSWORD

TREASURES IN HEAVEN

AVOIDING JEALOUSY OR GREED MEANS TAKING ON A DIFFERENT ATTITUDE. IT'S ABOUT DECIDING ON WHAT WILL HAVE MORE MEANING IN YOUR LIFE.

LET'S SEE WHAT GOD SAYS.

ACROSS
1. "DO NOT STORE UP FOR YOURSELVES _____ ON EARTH."
2. "WHERE MOTH AND _____ DESTROY."
3. "AND WHERE THIEVES BREAK IN AND _____."

MATTHEW 6:19

DOWN
1. "BUT STORE UP FOR _____."
2. "_____ IN HEAVEN."
3. "WHERE MOTH AND RUST DO NOT _____."
4. "AND WHERE _____ DO NOT BREAK IN AND STEAL."
5. "FOR WHERE YOUR TREASURE IS, THERE YOUR _____ WILL BE ALSO."

MATTHEW 6:20-21

310

311

DOUBLE *the* FUN

UNSCRAMBLE THE UNDERLINED WORDS IN
EACH VERSE. ON THE NEXT PAGE, PLACE YOUR
ANSWERS IN THE SPACES PROVIDED AND
THEN COMPLETE THE CROSSWORD PUZZLE.

SPEAKING TO THE RELIGIOUS LEADERS OF
HIS DAY, THE LORD MADE *VERY* CLEAR HIS
FEELINGS ON **GREED**.

1. "'WOE TO YOU, TEACHERS OF THE LAW
   AND EEPRSSAHI, YOU OPTRYSHECI! YOU
   LNACE THE OUTSIDE OF THE CUP AND
   HDSI, BUT INSIDE THEY ARE FULL OF
   GREED AND SELF-INDULGENCE.'"

   MATTHEW 23:25

2. "THEN THE LORD SAID TO HIM, 'NOW
   THEN, YOU PHARISEES CLEAN THE
   SUDOTEI OF THE CUP AND DISH, BUT
   NSIIED YOU ARE FULL OF REDEG AND
   WICKEDNESS.'"

   LUKE 11:39

1. __ __ __ __ __ __ __ __
__ __ __ __ __ __ __ __
__ __ __ __ __   __ __ __ __

2. __ __ __ __ __ __   __ __ __ __ __
__ __ __ __ __

SCRAMBLED VERSES

HAPPINESS

MANY CHASE AFTER HAPPINESS AS IF IT IS THE MOST IMPORTANT THING IN THE WORLD. USUALLY THOUGH, THEY END UP BEING THE MOST *UNHAPPY* PEOPLE AROUND!

HAPPINESS IS A *RESULT*...A RESULT OF MAKING THE RIGHT CHOICES IN LIFE AND LIVING THE KIND OF LIFE GOD WOULD WANT FOR YOU TO LIVE.

LOOK UP THE VERSE BELOW AND PUT THE WORDS IN THEIR PROPER ORDER TO FIND OUT MORE OF WHAT THE LORD SAYS ABOUT HAPPI-NESS.

GATHERING MAN MEANINGLESS, IS SINNER TOO PLEASES STORING TO WEALTH IT OVER AND UP THE "TO THE PLEASES WISDOM, GOD. WHO CHASING THE ONE WIND." HAPPINESS, HE GIVES OF HAND GOD THE TASK A AFTER BUT WHO HIM, KNOWLEDGE GIVES TO THE TO AND THIS

ECCLESIASTES 2:26

314

SECRET CODES

A GIFT OF GOD

REAL HAPPINESS COMES FROM GOD FIRST AND WITH WHATEVER HE MAY GIVE IN YOUR LIFE. THIS IS TO BE ENJOYED AS A GRACIOUS GIFT.

TO SOLVE THE CODED VERSE BELOW, LOOK AT EACH LETTER AND WRITE THE ONE THAT COMES BEFORE IT IN THE ALPHABET.

"NPSFPWFS, XIFO HPE HJWFT BOZ NBO XFBMUI BOE QPTTFTTJPOT, BOE FOBCMFT IJN UP FOKPZ UIFN, UP BDDFQU IJT MPU BOE CF IBQQZ JO IJT XPSL — UIJT JT B HJGU PG HPE."

ECCLESIASTES 5:19

316

A B C D E F G H I J K L M N O P Q R S T
U V W X Y Z

"_____ _____, _____

_____ _____ _____

_____ _____

_____ _____ _____,

_____ _____

_____ _____ _____

_____, _____ _____

_____ _____ _____

_____ _____ _____

_____ _____ _ _____

_____ _____ _____

_____."

FINISH *the* VERSE

A DIFFERENT KIND OF GIFT

DON'T THINK THAT EVERY GIFT IS GIVEN TO YOU FOR YOUR PLEASURE. SOME OF GOD'S GIFTS TO YOU ARE FOR OTHERS.

USE THE CODE CHART BELOW TO FINISH THE VERSE. (EG: K=24)

	1	2	3	4	5	6	7
1	A	B	C	D	E	F	G
2	H	I	J	K	L	M	N
3	O	P	Q	R	S	T	U
4	V	W	X	Y	Z		

"EACH ____ ____ ____   ____ ____ ____ ____ ____ ____
       31 27 15   35 21 31 37 25 14

USE ____ ____ ____ ____ ____ ____ ____ ____
    42   21   11 36 15 41 15 34

____ ____ ____ ____   HE   HAS   ____ ____ -
17   22 16   36   34   15

____ ____ ____ ____ ____ ____   TO   ____ ____ ____ ____ ____
13   15 22 41 15 14   35 15 34 41 15

____ ____ ____ ____ ____ ____,   FAITHFULLY
31   36 21   15 34 35

____ ____ ____ ____ ____ ____ ____ ____ ____ ____ ____ ____ ____
11   14 26 22 27 22 35 36 15 34 22 27 17

GOD'S ____ ____ ____ ____ ____   IN   ITS
      17   34 11 13 15

____ ____ ____ ____ ____ ____ ____   ____ ____ ____ ____ ____
41   11 34 22 31 37 35   16 31 34 26 35

1 PETER 4:10

CROSSWORD

HOPE IN GOD

EVEN WHEN YOU FEEL SO LOW, *LOOK TO GOD!*
SOON, HE WILL LIFT YOU UP. **COUNT ON IT!**

ACROSS
1. "WHY ARE YOU _____."
2. "O MY _____?"
3. "WHY SO _____ WITHIN ME?"
4. "PUT YOUR _____ IN GOD."
5. "FOR I WILL YET PRAISE HIM, MY SAVIOR AND MY _____."

DOWN
1. "MY SOUL IS _____ WITHIN ME."
2. "_____ I WILL REMEMBER YOU."
3. "FROM THE _____ OF THE JORDAN."
4. "THE HEIGHTS OF _____ —FROM MOUNT MIZAR."

PSALM 42:5-6

320

321

FILL *in the* BLANKS

GIVE THANKS

FINALLY, FINDING *TRUE* HAPPINESS DEPENDS
ON *YOUR* ATTITUDE TOWARDS EVERYTHING
IN YOUR LIFE. WHAT'S THE BEST WAY OF
DOING THIS?

USING THE WORDS BELOW, COMPLETE THE
VERSES ON THE NEXT PAGE AND YOU'LL SOON
FIND OUT!

HEART	LORD
SING	NAME
FATHER	MUSIC
MAKE	THANKS
LORD	EVERYTHING
JESUS	GIVING
GOD	CHRIST

"_____ AND _____ _____

IN YOUR _____ TO THE

_____, ALWAYS _____

_____ TO _____ THE

_____ FOR _____,

IN THE _____ OF OUR _____

_____ _____."

EPHESIANS 5:19-20

FINISH *the* VERSE

LONELINESS

IT CAN BE AWFUL, AT TIMES, TO FEEL THAT
YOU ARE ALL ALONE; WHEN YOUR FAMILY
SEEMS SO BUSY OR WHEN FRIENDS ARE NOT
THERE FOR YOU.

BUT, YOU HAVE A **FRIEND** THAT IS ALWAYS
WITH YOU AND WITH *HIM,* YOU NEVER NEED
TO FEEL LONELY AGAIN!

USE THE CODE CHART BELOW TO FINISH THE
VERSES. (EG: K=24)

	1	2	3	4	5	6	7
1	A	B	C	D	E	F	G
2	H	I	J	K	L	M	N
3	O	P	Q	R	S	T	U
4	V	W	X	Y	Z		

"TO ___ ___ ___, O ___ ___ ___ ___, I
    44 31 37   25 31 34 14

___ ___ ___ ___ ___ UP ___ ___   ___ ___ ___ ___."
25 22 16 36   26 44   35 31 37 25

PSALM 25:1

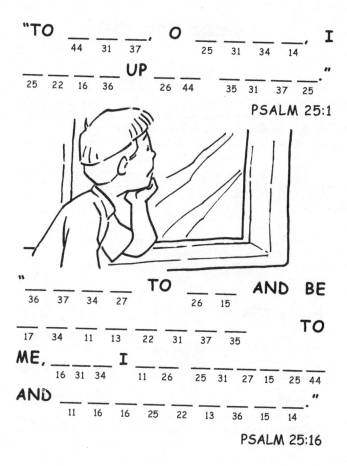

" ___ ___ ___ ___   TO   ___ ___   AND   BE
  36 37 34 27   26 15

___ ___ ___ ___ ___ ___ ___ ___   TO
17 34 11 13 22 31 37 35

ME, ___ ___ ___   I   ___ ___   ___ ___ ___ ___ ___ ___
     16 31 34   11 26   25 31 27 15 25 44

AND ___ ___ ___ ___ ___ ___ ___ ___ ___."
      11 16 16 25 22 13 36 15 14

PSALM 25:16

325

WORD SEARCH

GOD'S CHILDREN...*LONELY?*

IF YOU'RE GOD'S CHILD, HE HAS AN ANSWER FOR LONELINESS. LOOK UP **PSALM 68:6** IN YOUR BIBLE AND YOU'LL FIND OUT WHAT IT IS.

THEN, FIND THE WORDS, LISTED BELOW, IN THE WORD SEARCH ON THE NEXT PAGE.

LIVE

FAMILIES

LONELY

LEADS

LAND

REBELLIOUS

SETS

GOD

SINGING

SUN-SCORCHED

PRISONERS

FORTH

```
T H G T B Z S G D P L W
F Q S I N G I N G G O D
D M B L R X C L O F N N
K S F J E S Q G S H E P
F R U W D A I M R K L R
T R C N L I D S W S Y I
B E P V S E T S P N G S
K B Q L E C Q K D P C O
H E J N I I O R H T F N
M L G Z L J I R Q H L E
L L V R I L D T C Z T R
H I D F M B N L K H Z S
T O V Y A R X F P F E P
S U N E F O R T H T R D
W S C V S N T D N A L G
```

COLOR *the* PICTURE

A FANTASTIC PROMISE!

"AND SURELY I AM WITH YOU ALWAYS, TO THE VERY END OF THE AGE."

MATTHEW 28:20

JESUS HAS PROMISED TO NEVER LEAVE US. NO MATTER WHERE WE ARE OR WHAT WE DO, HE IS *ALWAYS* THERE WITH US.

THE LORD KNOWS OUR NEEDS AND UNDER-STANDS THAT WE NEED COMPANIONSHIP, SO HE HAS GIVEN US OUR FAMILY AND HE HAS GIVEN US FRIENDS.

HE IS SO WORTHY OF OUR PRAISE AND GRATITUDE!

DOUBLE *the* FUN

UNSCRAMBLE THE UNDERLINED WORDS IN
EACH VERSE. ON THE NEXT PAGE, PLACE YOUR
ANSWERS IN THE SPACES PROVIDED AND
THEN COMPLETE THE CROSSWORD PUZZLE.

1. "I WILL LIE DOWN AND SLEEP IN <u>CPEEA</u>,
   FOR YOU ALONE, O LORD, MAKE ME DWELL
   IN <u>YFESAT</u>."

   PSALM 4:8

2. "THE LORD <u>VSIGE</u> STRENGTH TO HIS
   PEOPLE; THE LORD <u>EBESLSS</u> HIS <u>LPOEPE</u>
   WITH PEACE."

   PSALM 29:11

3. "TURN FROM EVIL AND DO <u>ODOG</u>; <u>EKSE</u>
   PEACE AND <u>URPESU</u> IT."

   PSALM 34:14

1. _ _ _ _ _   _ _ _ _ _

2. _ _ _ _ _   _ _ _ _ _ _

_ _ _ _ _ _

3. _ _ _ _   _ _ _ _

_ _ _ _ _ _ _

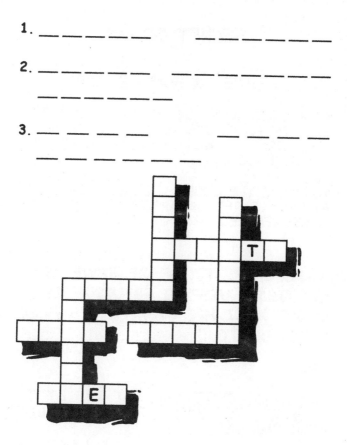

SECRET CODES

PEACE...A WAY OF LIFE

IT BEGINS WITH BEING AT PEACE WITH
GOD. IN HAVING A RELATIONSHIP WITH
THE LORD, HE WOULD LIKE FOR YOU TO
KNOW PEACE WITH THOSE IN YOUR LIFE.

TO SOLVE THE CODED VERSES BELOW, LOOK
AT EACH LETTER AND WRITE THE ONE THAT
COMES BEFORE IT IN THE ALPHABET.

"UIFSFGPSF, TJODF XF IBWF CFFO
KVTUJGJFE UISPVHI GBJUI, XF IBWF
QFBDF XJUI HPE UISPVHI PVS MPSE
KFTVT DISJTU."

ROMANS 5:1

and,

"JG JU JT QPTTJCMF, BT GBS BT JU
EFQFOET PO ZPV, MJWF BU QFBDF
XJUI FWFSZPOF."

ROMANS 12:18

ABCDEFGHIJKLMNOPQRST
UVWXYZ

CROSSWORD

SOWING PEACE

ACROSS
1. " BUT THE _____."
2. "THAT COMES FROM _____."
3. "IS FIRST OF ALL _____."
4. "THEN _____ -LOVING, CONSIDERATE."

DOWN
1. "_____, FULL OF MERCY AND
   GOOD FRUIT."
2. "IMPARTIAL AND _____."
3. "PEACEMAKERS WHO SOW IN _____."
4. "RAISE A _____ OF RIGHTEOUSNESS."

JAMES 3:17-18

334

FILL *in the* BLANKS

PEACE RULES!

ASK JESUS TO *RULE* IN YOUR HEART, TO BE LORD IN YOUR LIFE, AND YOU WILL KNOW HIS PEACE. THEN, **HIS** PEACE WILL FLOW OUT OF YOU TO OTHERS.

USING THE WORDS BELOW, COMPLETE THE VERSES ON THE NEXT PAGE AND YOU'LL KNOW WHAT TO DO.

QUARRELS	FOOLISH
PEACE	MEMBERS
RIGHTEOUSNESS	DESIRES
FLEE	ARGUMENTS
LORD	PURSUE
LOVE	HEART
YOUTH	PEACE
CHRIST	BODY
HEARTS	PEACE

"LET THE _____ OF _____
RULE IN YOUR _____, SINCE
AS _____ OF ONE _____
YOU WERE CALLED TO _____."

COLOSSIANS 3:15

"_____ THE EVIL _____ OF
_____, AND _____
_____, FAITH,
_____ AND _____, ALONG
WITH THOSE WHO CALL ON THE
_____ OUT OF A PURE _____.
DON'T HAVE ANYTHING TO DO WITH
_____ AND STUPID
_____, BECAUSE YOU
KNOW THEY PRODUCE _____."

2 TIMOTHY 2:22-23

FILL THEM IN

DON'T BE ANXIOUS!

LOOK UP PHILIPPIANS 4:6-7 IN YOUR BIBLE.

ON THE NEXT PAGE, FILL IN THE BOXES WITH WHAT YOU NEED TO DO AND WHAT YOU WILL RECEIVE.

SCRAMBLED VERSES

TAKE HEART!

GOD GIVES SO MUCH. THE PEACE THAT HE LEAVES WITH US IS ONE OF THE BEST THINGS WE CAN HAVE. TO BE FREE OF ANXI-ETY AND WORRY IS A WONDERFUL FEELING.

UNSCRAMBLE THE VERSES BELOW AND BE ASSURED!

"CEEPA I EVLAE WHTI UYO; YM PCAEE I IGVE OYU. I OD TON VIEG OT YOU SA HET LWRDO IESGV. OD TNO TLE OYRU THAERS EB UOEDBTLR NDA OD ONT EB AAIFDR."

"I AVHE DTLO OUY SEEHT SHIGNT, OS HATT NI EM UYO YMA AVHE CEAPE. NI SITH ODRWL UYO LILW AEVH BLRTEUO. TBU TEKA ARHET! I EAVH COEORVEM HET DWLOR."

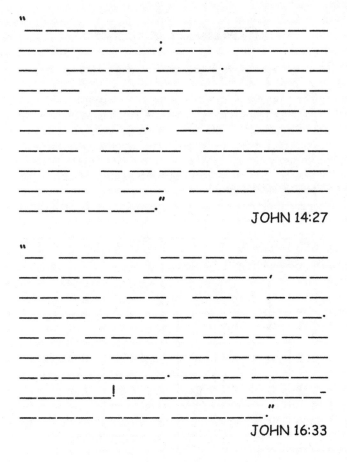

"_____ __ _____
_____ _____; ___ _____
__ _____ ____. _ ___
___ _____ ___ ____
___ ____ ___ _____
_____. ___ ____
____ _____ _____
__ __ ____ ____ __
___ ___ ___ ___
_____."

JOHN 14:27

"_ ____ ____ ___
____ _____,' __
____ __ __ ____
___ ____ ___ ____.
__ ___ ____ ___
___ _____ ___ _
_____! _ _____ ____-
____ ___ _____."

JOHN 16:33

341

FINISH *the* VERSE

TEMPTATION!

DOES A DAY GO BY WHERE THERE ISN'T A TEMPTATION TO DO SOMETHING WRONG OR TO REACT IN THE WRONG WAY?

YOU WANT TO LIVE RIGHT...YOU WANT TO DO AS GOD WOULD HAVE YOU DO, BUT SOME-TIMES, IT ALMOST SEEMS IMPOSSIBLE. IS THERE *ANY* HELP?

LET'S LOOK TO GOD'S WORD, ONCE AGAIN.

USE THE CODE CHART BELOW TO FINISH THE VERSE. (EG: K=24)

	1	2	3	4	5	6	7
1	A	B	C	D	E	F	G
2	H	I	J	K	L	M	N
3	O	P	Q	R	S	T	U
4	V	W	X	Y	Z		

342

"WHEN ___ ___ ___ ___ ___ ___ ___, NO ONE
36 15 26 32 36 15 14

___ ___ ___ ___ ___ ___ SAY, 'GOD IS
35 21 31 37 25 14

___ ___ ___ ___ ___ ___ ___ ___ ME.' FOR GOD
36 15 26 32 36 22 27 17

___ ___ ___ ___ ___ ___ BE ___ ___ ___ ___ ___ ___
13 11 27 27 31 36   36 15 26 32 36 15 14

BY ___ ___ ___ ___, NOR DOES HE ___ ___ ___ ___ ___
   15 41 22 25   36 15 26 32 36

___ ___ ___ ___ ___ ___; BUT ___ ___ ___ ___ ONE
11 27 44 31 27 15   15 11 13 21

IS ___ ___ ___ ___ ___ ___ WHEN, BY HIS
   36 15 26 32 36 15 14

___ ___ ___ ___ ___ ___ ___ ___ ___ ___ ___ ___ ___,
31 42 27   15 41 22 25   14 15 35 22 34 15

HE IS ___ ___ ___ ___ ___ ___ AWAY
      14 34 11 17 17 15 14

AND ___ ___ ___ ___ ___ ___ ___. THEN,
    15 27 36 22 13 15 14

AFTER ___ ___ ___ ___ ___ ___ HAS
      14 15 35 22 34 15

___ ___ ___ ___ ___ ___ ___ ___, IT GIVES
13 31 27 13 15 22 41 15 14

___ ___ ___ ___ ___ ___ TO ___ ___ ___; AND SIN,
12 22 34 36 21   35 22 27

WHEN IT IS ___ ___ ___ ___ ___ - ___ ___ ___ ___ ___,
           16 37 25 25   17 34 31 42 27

GIVES ___ ___ ___ ___ ___ ___ TO ___ ___ ___ ___ ___ ___."
      12 22 34 36 21   14 15 11 36 21

JAMES 1:13-15

WORD SEARCH

STAND AGAINST TEMPTATION

DOES GOD HAVE A WAY FOR YOU TO RESIST
TEMPTATION?

FIND THE WORDS UNDERLINED BELOW IN THE
WORD SEARCH ON THE NEXT PAGE.

"NO <u>TEMPTATION</u> HAS <u>SEIZED</u> YOU
<u>EXCEPT</u> WHAT IS <u>COMMON</u> TO <u>MAN</u>.
AND <u>GOD</u> IS <u>FAITHFUL</u>; HE WILL NOT
LET YOU BE <u>TEMPTED</u> <u>BEYOND</u> WHAT
YOU CAN <u>BEAR</u>. BUT WHEN YOU ARE
TEMPTED, HE WILL ALSO <u>PROVIDE</u> A
<u>WAY</u> OUT SO THAT YOU CAN <u>STAND</u>
UP <u>UNDER</u> IT."

1 CORINTHIANS 10:13

```
X R Z G O D R L F R N J
F W D G S E I Z E D L Z
B H J T P D T H T R W K
E K L D E S E L H A B T
A M T N C M M M Y T L C
R B H N R T P S D U R M
F R Q P D T T T F F D P
S T A N D K A H E H X E
B E J J N L T B C D M X
K D T K B I I N T U R C
H I L T A D O N D N G E
L V T F N M N N Q D Z P
T O C V M J A T D E L T
H R P O H L G N K R T X
T P C R B B E Y O N D S
```

MULTIPLE CHOICE

"PEOPLE WHO WANT TO GET RICH FALL INTO TEMPTATION AND A TRAP AND INTO MANY FOOLISH AND HARMFUL DESIRES THAT PLUNGE MEN INTO RUIN AND DESTRUCTION."

1 TIMOTHY 6:9

AFTER READING THE VERSE ABOVE, WHAT WOULD BE THE RIGHT CHOICES BELOW?

1. YOU GET A LOT OF MONEY FOR YOUR BIRTH-DAY.
   - A) YOU HIDE IT AWAY, SO YOU DON'T EVER HAVE TO SHARE.
   - B) YOU GIVE SOME BACK TO GOD, PUT SOME TOWARDS SAVINGS, AND TAKE A LITTLE TO SPEND.
   - C) YOU SPEND IT ALL AT THE LOCAL VIDEO ARCADE.

2. YOUR YOUNGER BROTHER'S BIKE HAS A FLAT
   TIRE AND HE HAS NO MONEY TO REPAIR IT.
      A) YOU OFFER TO LOAN HIM THE MONEY
         AND HE CAN PAY IT BACK WHEN HE
         CAN.
      B) YOU TELL HIM TO TAKE CARE OF HIS
         OWN PROBLEMS.
      C) YOU GIVE HIM THE MONEY AS LONG
         AS HE CLEANS YOUR ROOM FOR THE
         NEXT YEAR.

3. YOU FINALLY GOT THAT NEW GAME SYSTEM!
      A) YOU SHARE IT WITH NO ONE.
      B) YOU SPEND ALL YOUR TIME AT IT...
         YOUR CHORES AREN'T GETTING DONE
         AND YOUR GRADES ARE SLIPPING.
      C) YOU CAREFULLY SCHEDULE YOUR
         TIME ON IT.

4. YOU'VE BEEN ASKED AT CHURCH TO GIVE TO
   AN EMERGENCY RELIEF FUND.
      A) YOU GIVE TEN PERCENT OF YOUR
         SAVINGS.
      B) YOU'RE ANGRY BUT GIVE BECAUSE IT
         IS EXPECTED OF YOU.
      C) YOU ASK GOD WHAT AMOUNT HE
         WOULD HAVE YOU GIVE.

SECRET CODES

WE WILL FIND MERCY AND HELP

BE CONFIDENT! NO MATTER WHAT YOU'VE DONE, IT DOESN'T CHANGE GOD'S LOVE FOR YOU. YOU *CAN* GO TO HIM AND FIND THAT HIS FORGIVENESS IS ALWAYS THERE FOR YOU. HE WILL GIVE THE STRENGTH YOU NEED TO WITHSTAND TEMPTATION.

TO SOLVE THE CODED VERSES BELOW, LOOK AT EACH LETTER AND WRITE THE ONE THAT COMES BEFORE IT IN THE ALPHABET.

"CFDBVTF IF IJNTFMG TVGGFSFE XIFO IF XBT UFNQUFE, IF JT BCMF UP IFMQ UIPTF XIP BSF CFJOH UFNQUFE."

HEBREWS 2:18

"MFU VT UIFO BQQSPBDI UIF UISPOF PG HSBDF XJUI DPOGJEFODF, TP UIBU XF NBZ SFDFJWF NFSDZ BOE GJOE HSBDF UP IFMQ VT JO PVS UJNF PG OFFE."

HEBREWS 4:16

348

ABCDEFGHIJKLMNOPQRST
UVWXYZ

FILL *in the* BLANKS

WATCH YOURSELF!

NOT ONLY DO WE DEAL WITH OUR OWN SIN, BUT THERE ARE THE SINS OF OTHERS THAT MAY AFFECT US IN SOME WAY. HOW DO WE HANDLE THAT?

USING THE WORDS BELOW, COMPLETE THE VERSE ON THE NEXT PAGE AND YOU'LL KNOW WHAT TO DO.

WATCH	BROTHERS
TEMPTED	RESTORE
CAUGHT	GENTLY
SOMEONE	ALSO
SPIRITUAL	SIN
YOURSELF	SHOULD

"_____, IF _____
IS _____ IN A _____, YOU
WHO ARE _____
_____ _____ HIM
_____. BUT _____
_____, OR YOU _____
MAY BE _____."

GALATIANS 6:1

CROSSWORD

PATIENCE

THEY SAY, "PATIENCE IS A VIRTUE"...AND IT IS, BUT SOMETIMES, IT SURE SEEMS TO BE A VERY DIFFICULT THING TO DO!

ACROSS

1. "_____ AS AN EXAMPLE OF PATIENCE."
2. "IN THE FACE OF _____."
3. "TAKE THE _____ WHO SPOKE."
4. "IN THE _____ OF THE LORD."

DOWN

1. "AS YOU KNOW, WE CONSIDER _____."
2. "THOSE WHO HAVE _____."
3. "YOU HAVE HEARD OF _____ PERSEVERANCE."
4. "AND HAVE _____ WHAT THE LORD FINALLY BROUGHT ABOUT."
5. "THE LORD IS FULL OF COMPASSION AND _____."

JAMES 5:10-11

352

FILL THEM IN

AN EXAMPLE

AFTER GETTING THROUGH THESE VERSES, YOU MIGHT FIND IT A LITTLE EASIER TO BE PATIENT ABOUT THE THINGS THAT MAY HAPPEN IN YOUR LIFE.

LOOK UP 2 CORINTHIANS 6:3-6 IN YOUR BIBLE.

ON THE NEXT PAGE, FILL IN THE BOXES WITH THESE EXAMPLES OF SUFFERINGS AND GODLY RESPONSES.

354

FINISH *the* VERSE

PATIENT SALVATION

GOD'S PATIENCE HAS MEANT FOR US, OUR SALVATION. SURELY, THE LORD WOULD WANT US TO SHOW OTHERS PATIENCE WHEN THEY DISAPPOINT US.

USE THE CODE CHART BELOW TO FINISH THE VERSE. (EG: K=24)

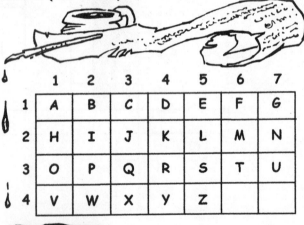

	1	2	3	4	5	6	7
1	A	B	C	D	E	F	G
2	H	I	J	K	L	M	N
3	O	P	Q	R	S	T	U
4	V	W	X	Y	Z		

" __ __ __ __ IN __ __ __ __ THAT
  12 15 11 34   26 22 27 14

OUR __ __ __ __ ' __ __ __-
      25 31 34 14 35   32 11

__ __ __ __ __ __ MEANS __ __ __-
36 22 15 27 13 15   35 11 25

__ __ __ __ __ __, JUST AS OUR
41 11 36 22 31 27

DEAR __ __ __ __ __ __ __
      12 34 31 36 21 15 34

__ __ __ __ ALSO __ __ __ __ __
32 11 37 25   42 34 31 36 15

YOU WITH THE __ __ __ __ __ __
              42 22 35 14 31 26

THAT __ __ __ GAVE HIM."
      17 31 14

2 PETER 3:15

357

COLOR *the* PICTURE

A LAST WORD

THE APOSTLE PAUL SPOKE TO ALL OF US IN PHILIPPIANS 2:14–18 AND THEY ARE GOOD WORDS TO LEAVE YOU WITH.

MAY GOD'S BLESSINGS GO WITH YOU.

"DO EVERYTHING WITHOUT COMPLAINING OR ARGUING, SO THAT YOU MAY BECOME BLAMELESS AND PURE, CHILDREN OF GOD WITHOUT FAULT IN A CROOKED AND DEPRAVED GENERATION, IN WHICH YOU SHINE LIKE STARS IN THE UNIVERSE AS YOU HOLD OUT THE WORD OF LIFE—IN ORDER THAT I MAY BOAST ON THE DAY OF CHRIST THAT I DID NOT RUN OR LABOR FOR NOTHING. BUT EVEN IF I AM BEING POURED OUT LIKE A DRINK OFFERING ON THE SACRIFICE AND SERVICE COMING FROM YOUR FAITH, I AM GLAD AND REJOICE WITH ALL OF YOU. SO YOU TOO SHOULD BE GLAD AND REJOICE WITH ME."

≡ANSWER PAGES≡

PG. 197

```
H R Q L Y V D M F K F W
F J G O N C L G A E F B
G S J V B T B X B W A I
A D B E B D F L X O T R
P N T E L Q S O R F D
T P G R B W C X U R S X
R Z T E R V D H V Y S G
W A C T R B D M D M E W
H A P P I N E S S P N L
Q L R V B J D Z B D I D
M W I B B B E K C F L Q
B Y D N B C T W T H E J
T C E P A Q N S N K N W
N M J E B V S M Q B O P
K R P D B R D G U I L T
```

PG. 199

"LET US THEN __APPROACH__
THE __THRONE__ OF GRACE WITH
__CONFIDENCE__ , SO THAT WE MAY
__RECEIVE__   __MERCY__ AND FIND
__GRACE__ TO __HELP__ US IN OUR
__TIME__ OF __NEED__ ."   HEBREWS 4:16

PG. 201

"__C O M E__   __T O__   __M E__,
__A L L__   __Y O U__   __W H O__
__A R E__   __W E A R__ Y   __A N D__
__B U R D E N E D__,   __A N D__
__I__   __W I L L__   __G I V E__
__Y O U__   __R E S T__.   __T A K E__
__M Y__   __Y O K E__   __U P O N__
__Y O U__   __A N D__   __L E A R N__
__F R O M__   __M E__,   __F O R__   __I__
__A M__   __G E N T L E__   __A N D__
__H U M B L E__   __I N__
__H E A R T__,   __A N D__   __Y O U__
__W I L L__   __F I N D__ __R E S T__
__F O R__   __Y O U R__   __S O U L S__.
__F O R__   __M Y__   __Y O K E__   __I S__
__E A S Y__   __A N D__ __M Y__   __B U R-__
__D E N__   __I S__   __L I G H T__."
                         MATTHEW 11:28-30

360

ABCDEFGHIJKLMNOPQRS
TUVWXYZ

"F O R   T H E   W A G E S
O F   S I N   I S
D E A T H,   B U T
T H E G I F T   O F
G O D   I S   E T E R-
N A L   L I F E   I N
C H R I S T   J E S U S
O U R   L O R D."

ROMANS 6:23

"SO I $\underset{35}{S} \underset{11}{A} \underset{44}{Y},$ $\underset{25}{L} \underset{22}{I} \underset{41}{V} \underset{15}{E}$

BY THE $\underset{35}{S} \underset{32}{P} \underset{22}{I} \underset{34}{R} \underset{22}{I} \underset{36}{T},$ AND

YOU $\underset{42}{W} \underset{22}{I} \underset{25}{L} \underset{25}{L}$ NOT

$\underset{17}{G} \underset{34}{R} \underset{11}{A} \underset{36}{T} \underset{22}{I} \underset{16}{F} \underset{44}{Y}$ THE

$\underset{14}{D} \underset{15}{E} \underset{35}{S} \underset{22}{I} \underset{34}{R} \underset{15}{E} \underset{35}{S}$ OF THE

$\underset{35}{S} \underset{22}{I} \underset{27}{N} \underset{16}{F} \underset{37}{U} \underset{25}{L}$ $\underset{27}{N} \underset{11}{A} \underset{36}{T} \underset{37}{U} \underset{34}{R} \underset{15}{E}."$

GALATIANS 5:16

361

1. B E D S   H E A R T S
2. A N G E R   M O M E N T
3. F O R G A V E   T I M E
    W R A T H

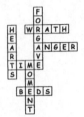

PG. 212

MULTIPLE CHOICE

ANGER IS JUST A FEELING, BUT IT IS WHAT YOU DO WITH IT THAT CAN MAKE IT RIGHT OR WRONG.

1. YOUR BROTHER CALLS YOU A NAME. WHAT SHOULD YOU DO?
   A) CALL HIM AN EVEN NASTIER NAME.
   B) TELL HIM THAT WASN'T NICE AND THAT YOU DIDN'T LIKE IT.
   C) IGNORE HIM AND DON'T SPEAK TO HIM AGAIN.

2. YOU WANT TO STAY OVERNIGHT AT A FRIEND'S HOUSE. YOUR PARENTS SAY NO.
   A) YOU SHOULD ARGUE WITH THEM.
   B) YOU SHOULD HAVE A TEMPER TANTRUM.
   C) YOU SHOULD ACCEPT THEIR ANSWER AND MAKE OTHER PLANS.

3. A FRIEND SHARES HER CANDY WITH EVERYONE ELSE, BUT LEAVES YOU OUT.
   A) CALL HER NAMES.
   B) TALK ABOUT HER BEHIND HER BACK.
   C) TELL HER PRIVATELY HOW YOU FEEL.

PG. 213

4. JUST BEFORE IT'S YOUR TURN IN THE HOT DOG LINE, SOMEONE BUTTS IN FRONT OF YOU.
   A) YELL AT THEM AND TELL THEM YOU'RE NEXT.
   B) POLITELY TELL THEM YOU ARE NEXT.
   C) PUSH THEM OUT OF THE WAY.

5. THE TEACHER EMBARRASSES YOU IN FRONT OF THE CLASS.
   A) TALK POLITELY WITH THE TEACHER AFTER CLASS.
   B) EMBARRASS THE TEACHER BACK.
   C) AFTER CLASS, PUT TACKS ON THE TEACHER'S CHAIR.

6. YOU SEE A GROUP OF KIDS PICKING ON YOUR FRIEND.
   A) RUN IN WITH FISTS FLYING.
   B) GO TO AN ADULT FOR HELP.
   C) GO STAND BESIDE YOUR FRIEND.

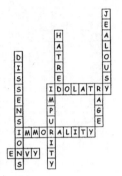

PG. 217

"IN YOUR ANGER
DO NOT SIN: DO
NOT LET THE SUN
GO DOWN WHILE
YOU ARE STILL
ANGRY, AND DO
NOT GIVE THE
DEVIL A FOOT-
HOLD."

"GET RID OF ALL
BITTERNESS,
RAGE AND ANGER,
BRAWLING AND
SLANDER, ALONG
WITH EVERY
FORM OF MALICE.
BE KIND AND
COMPASSIONATE
TO ONE ANOTHER,
FORGIVING EACH
OTHER, JUST AS
IN CHRIST GOD
FORGAVE YOU."

"A F O O L GIVES F U L L
   16 31 31 25   16 37 25 25

V E N T TO HIS A N G E R,
41 15 27 36   11 27 17 15 34

BUT A W I S E   M A N
       42 22 35 15 26 11 27

KEEPS   H I M S E L F
           21 27 26 35 15 25 16

UNDER   C O N T R O L."
         13 31 27 36 34 31 25

PROVERBS 29:11

"THEREFORE, AS GOD'S _CHOSEN_
PEOPLE, _HOLY_ AND DEARLY _LOVED_,
CLOTHE YOURSELVES WITH
COMPASSION, KINDNESS,
HUMILITY, _GENTLENESS_ AND
PATIENCE. _BEAR_ WITH EACH OTHER
AND _FORGIVE_ WHATEVER
GRIEVANCES YOU MAY _HAVE_
AGAINST ONE _ANOTHER_. FORGIVE
AS THE _LORD_ _FORGAVE_ YOU."

COLOSSIANS 3:12-13

"BLESS THOSE
WHO PERSECUTE
YOU; BLESS AND
DO NOT CURSE.
REJOICE WITH
THOSE WHO RE-
JOICE; MOURN
WITH THOSE WHO
MOURN. LIVE IN
HARMONY WITH
ONE ANOTHER.
DO NOT BE PROUD,
BUT BE WILLING
TO ASSOCIATE
WITH PEOPLE OF
LOW POSITION.
DO NOT BE CON-
CEITED."

ROMANS 12:14-16

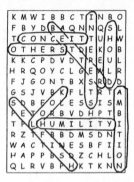

"BROTHERS, IF
  12 34 31 36 21 15 34 35
SOMEONE IS
35 31 26 15 31 27 15
CAUGHT IN A SIN, YOU
13 11 37 17 21 36   35 22 27
WHO ARE SPIRITUAL
          35 32 22 34 22 36 37 11 25
SHOULD RESTORE
15 21 31 37 25 14 34 15 35 36 31 34 15
HIM GENTLY. BUT
     17 15 27 36 25 44
WATCH YOURSELF, OR YOU
47 11 36 13 21
ALSO MAY BE TEMPTED.
11 25 35 31   36 15 76 32 36 15 14
CARRY EACH OTHER'S
13 11 34 34 44 15 11 13 21
BURDENS. AND IN THIS
12 37 34 14 15 27 35   36 21 27 35
WAY YOU WILL FULFILL
                  16 37 25 16 22 25 25
THE LAW OF CHRIST."
    25 11 42   13 21 34 22 35 36

GALATIANS 6:1-2

1. MERCY   LOVE

2. GRACIOUS
   RIGHTEOUS

3. LORD
   COMPASSION

```
L           C
O   RIGHTEOUS
R           M
D           P
    M       A
    E       S
  GRACIOUS  S
    C       I
    Y       LOVE
            N
```

364

ABCDEFGHIJKLMNOPQRST
UVWXYZ

"ABOVE ALL, LOVE
EACH OTHER
DEEPLY, BE-
CAUSE LOVE
COVERS OVER
A MULTITUDE OF
SINS. OFFER
HOSPITALITY
TO ONE ANOTHER
WITHOUT GRUMB-
LING."

1 PETER 4:8-9

" FINALLY, ALL OF YOU, LIVE
IN HARMONY WITH ONE
ANOTHER; BE SYMPATHETIC, LOVE
AS BROTHERS, BE COMPASSIONATE
AND HUMBLE. DO NOT REPAY
EVIL WITH EVIL OR INSULT WITH
INSULT, BUT WITH BLESSING,
BECAUSE TO THIS YOU WERE CALLED
SO THAT YOU MAY INHERIT A
BLESSING."

1 PETER 3:8-5

"THERE ARE SIX THINGS THE
LORD HATES,
SEVEN THAT ARE
DETESTABLE TO
HIM: HAUGHTY EYES, A
LYING TONGUE, HANDS
THAT SHED INNOCENT
BLOOD, A HEART THAT
DEVISES WICKED
SCHEMES, FEET
THAT ARE QUICK TO RUSH
INTO EVIL, A FALSE WITNESS
WHO POURS OUT LIES AND A
MAN WHO STIRS UP DIS-
SENSION AMONG
BROTHERS."

PROVERBS 6:16-19

"YOU ARE NOT A
GOD WHO TAKES
PLEASURE IN
EVIL; WITH YOU
THE WICKED CAN-
NOT DWELL. THE
ARROGANT CAN-
NOT STAND IN
YOUR PRESENCE;
YOU HATE ALL
WHO DO WRONG"

PSALM 5:4-5

"THERE IS A TIME
FOR EVERYTHING,
AND A SEASON FOR
EVERY ACTIVITY
UNDER HEAVEN."

ECCLESIASTES 3:1

"A TIME TO LOVE
AND A TIME TO
HATE."

ECCLESIASTES 3:8

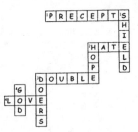

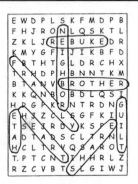

"BUT I _TELL_ YOU WHO _HEAR_
ME: _LOVE_ YOUR _ENEMIES_,
DO _GOOD_ TO THOSE WHO _HATE_
YOU, _BLESS_ THOSE WHO _CURSE_

366

HOW DOES GOD LOVE US?

"FOR <u>G O D</u> SO <u>L O V E D</u>
       17 31 14   25 31 41 15 14

THE <u>W O R L D</u> THAT HE
      42 31 34 25 14

<u>G A V E</u> <u>H I S</u> <u>O N E</u>
 31 11 41 15 21 22 35 31 27 15

AND <u>O N L Y</u> <u>S O N</u>, THAT
      31 27 25 44 35 31 27

<u>W H O E V E R</u> BELIEVES <u>I N</u>
 42 21 31 15 41 15 34   22 27

<u>H I M</u> <u>S H A L L</u> NOT
 21 22 26 35 21 11 25 25

<u>P E R I S H</u> BUT HAVE
 32 15 34 22 35 21

<u>E T E R N A L</u> <u>L I F E.</u>"
 15 36 15 34 27 11 25 25 22 16 15

JOHN 3:16

MAYBE, IF WE CHOOSE TO TREAT OTHERS KINDLY,
NO MATTER WHAT, OR WE DO AS ASKED, OUR *ACT*
OF OBEDIENCE DEMONSTRATES OUR LOVE!

A B C D E F G H I J K L M N O P Q R S T
U V W X Y Z

"<u>A</u> <u>N E W</u> <u>C O M M A N D</u>
<u>I</u> <u>G I V E</u> <u>Y O U</u>:
<u>L O V E</u> <u>O N E</u>
<u>A N O T H E R</u>. <u>A S</u> <u>I</u>
<u>H A V E</u> <u>L O V E D</u>
<u>Y O U</u>, <u>S O</u> <u>Y O U</u>
<u>M U S T</u> <u>L O V E</u> <u>O N E</u>
<u>A N O T H E R</u>. <u>B Y</u>
<u>T H I S</u> <u>A L L</u> <u>M E N</u>
<u>W I L L</u> <u>K N O W</u> <u>T H A T</u>
<u>Y O U</u> <u>A R E</u> <u>M Y</u> <u>D I S-</u>
<u>C I P L E S</u>. <u>I F</u> <u>Y O U</u>
<u>L O V E</u> <u>O N E</u> <u>A N O-</u>
<u>T H E R</u>."

JOHN 13:34-35

MULTIPLE CHOICE

"YOU HAVE HEARD THAT IT WAS SAID, 'LOVE
YOUR NEIGHBOR AND HATE YOUR ENEMY.'
BUT I TELL YOU: LOVE YOUR ENEMIES AND
PRAY FOR THOSE WHO PERSECUTE YOU."

MATTHEW 5:43-44

BASED ON THE VERSES ABOVE, WHAT SHOULD
BE DONE IN THE FOLLOWING SITUATIONS?

1. A GIRL AT SCHOOL HAS BEEN SPREADING
   LIES ABOUT YOU.
   A) CHALLENGE HER TO A FIGHT.
   B) INVITE HER TO YOUR HOUSE AND
      GET TO KNOW HER.
   C) REPORT HER TO THE PRINCIPAL.
2. SOMEONE STOLE YOUR BIKE AND YOU
   KNOW WHO IT IS.
   A) PHONE THE POLICE.
   B) ASK FOR IT BACK AND OFFER YOUR
      OLD BIKE FOR FREE.
   C) YOU AND YOUR BUDDIES SHOULD GO
      AND CONFRONT HIM.

3. SOMEONE YOU THOUGHT WAS YOUR
   FRIEND COPIED YOUR BOOK REPORT AND
   HAS BLAMED YOU FOR CHEATING.
   A) GOD REVEALS THE TRUTH AND YOU
      DECIDE YOU CAN NO LONGER BE
      FRIENDS.
   B) YOU TAKE THE BLAME.
   C) GOD REVEALS THE TRUTH AND YOU
      OFFER FORGIVENESS.
4. KIDS AT SCHOOL LAUGH AT YOU BECAUSE
   OF YOUR FAITH.
   A) IN THE FUTURE, YOU DECIDE TO
      KEEP YOUR FAITH A SECRET.
   B) YOU DECIDE TO USE THIS AS AN
      OPPORTUNITY TO SHARE YOUR
      FAITH.
   C) YOU BOLDLY CONFRONT THEM AND
      CONDEMN THEM FOR THEIR SIN.
5. JESUS WAS UNFAIRLY JUDGED AND SENT
   TO THE CROSS.
   A) HE ASKED HIS FATHER TO FORGIVE
      THOSE RESPONSIBLE, THEN DIED
      FOR US ALL.
   B) HE CALLED UPON LEGIONS OF
      ANGELS TO SAVE HIM.
   C) HE CRIED OUT FOR MERCY.

1. S T R E N G T H
2. G O O D N E S S   L O V E
   L I F E   D W E L L
   H O U S E
3. R E S T   H O P E

"B U T   L O V E   Y O U R
E N E M I E S,   D O   G O O D
T O   T H E M,   A N D
L E N D   T O   T H E M
W I T H O U T   E X-
P E C T I N G   T O   G E T
A N Y T H I N G   B A C K.
T H E N   Y O U R   R E-
W A R D   W I L L   B E
G R E A T,   A N D   Y O U
W I L L   B E   S O N S   O F
T H E   M O S T   H I G H,
B E C A U S E   H E   I S
K I N D   T O   T H E
U N G R A T E F U L
A N D   W I C K E D."

LUKE 6:35

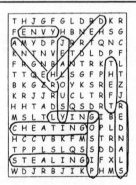

368

MULTIPLE CHOICE

"DO TO OTHERS AS YOU WOULD HAVE THEM
DO TO YOU."

LUKE 6:31

AFTER READING THE VERSE ABOVE, WHAT WOULD
BE THE RIGHT CHOICES BELOW?

1. PETER BETRAYED JESUS THE NIGHT OF HIS TRIAL.
   - A) JESUS FOREVER BANNED HIM FROM HEAVEN.
   - B) JESUS EXPECTED PETER TO MAKE IT UP TO HIM.
   - C) JESUS FORGAVE HIM.

2. JESUS TOLD OF A MAN WHO WAS FORGIVEN HIS DEBTS.
   - A) THE MAN WAS NOW FREE TO COLLECT FROM THOSE WHO OWED HIM.
   - B) HE SHOULD FORGIVE OTHERS THEIR DEBTS TO HIM.
   - C) HE SHOULD PAY IT BACK ANYWAY.

3. BOTH YOU AND YOUR FRIEND HAVE BEEN OFFERED THE SAME ROLE IN THE SCHOOL PLAY.
   - A) DO YOUR BEST AT THE AUDITION.
   - B) OFFER A BRIBE TO GET THE PART.
   - C) DECLINE THE PART.

4. JESUS TOLD OF A FATHER WHO WAITED FOR A REBELLIOUS SON TO RETURN HOME.
   - A) THE FATHER SHOULD WELCOME HIM BACK AND CELEBRATE.
   - B) HE SHOULD NOT ALLOW THE SON BACK UNTIL HE PAYS BACK THE MONEY HE SQUANDERED.
   - C) HE SHOULD TAKE HIM BACK BUT TREAT HIM AS ONE OF HIS SERVANTS.

5. AN INJURED MAN LIES ON THE SIDE OF THE ROAD.
   - A) PASS BY, HOPING SOMEONE ELSE WILL TAKE CARE OF HIM.
   - B) MAKE HIM COMFORTABLE, THEN RUN FOR HELP.
   - C) CHECK HIS CLOTHING FOR ANY VALUABLES.

6. YOUR PARENTS HAVE ASKED A FAVOR, THAT YOU WOULD CLEAN THE CARS.
   - A) YOU AGREE BUT DECIDE LATER NOT TO BOTHER.
   - B) YOU WILL....AS LONG AS THEY PAY YOU.
   - C) YOU DO IT WILLINGLY, REALIZING HOW MUCH THEY DO FOR YOU.

"IF YOU <u>L O V E</u> THOSE WHO
⎯25 31 41 15

<u>L O V E</u> YOU, WHAT <u>C R E D I T</u>
⎯25 31 41 15   13 34 15 14 22 36

IS <u>T H A T</u> TO YOU? EVEN
⎯36 21 11 36

'<u>S I N N E R S</u>' <u>L O V E</u>
⎯35 22 27 27 15 34 35   25 31 41 15

<u>T H O S E</u> WHO <u>L O V E</u>
⎯36 21 31 35 15   25 31 41 15

THEM. AND IF YOU DO <u>G O O D</u> TO
⎯17 31 31 14

<u>T H O S E</u> WHO ARE <u>G O O D</u>
⎯36 21 31 35 15   17 31 31 14

TO YOU, WHAT <u>C R E D I T</u> IS
⎯13 34 15 14 22 36

THAT TO <u>Y O U</u>? EVEN
⎯44 31 37

'<u>S I N N E R S</u>' DO THAT.
⎯35 22 27 27 15 34 35

LUKE 6:32-33

369

" DO NOT GLOAT WHEN
YOUR ENEMY FALLS ;
WHEN HE STUMBLES ,
DO NOT LET YOUR
HEART REJOICE ."

" BLESS THOSE WHO
PERSECUTE YOU;
BLESS AND DO NOT
CURSE ."

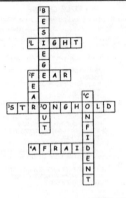

"KEEP YOUR LIVES FREE
FROM THE LOVE OF MONEY
AND BE CONTENT WITH
WHAT YOU HAVE . BECAUSE
GOD HAS SAID, ' NEVER WILL
I LEAVE YOU ; NEVER WILL
I FORSAKE YOU. '"
                              HEBREWS 13:5

A B C D E F G H I J K L M N O P Q R S T
       U V W X Y Z
"CAST YOUR CARES
ON THE LORD AND
HE WILL SUSTAIN
YOU; HE WILL
NEVER LET THE
RIGHTEOUS FALL"

"BUT YOU, O GOD,
WILL BRING DOWN
THE WICKED INTO
THE PIT OF COR-
RUPTION; BLOOD-
THIRSTY AND
DECEITFUL MEN
WILL NOT LIVE
OUT HALF THEIR
DAYS. BUT AS FOR
ME, I TRUST IN
YOU."

1. F E A R   P U R E
   F O R E V E R
   O R D I N A N C E S

2. W A L K   V A L L E Y
   S H A D O W   E V I L
   R O D   C O M F O R T

" THEREFORE I TELL
YOU, DO NOT WORRY
ABOUT YOUR LIFE,
WHAT YOU WILL EAT
OR DRINK; OR ABOUT
YOUR BODY, WHAT
YOU WILL WEAR.
IS NOT LIFE MORE
IMPORTANT THAN
FOOD, AND THE BODY
MORE IMPORTANT
THAN CLOTHES ?"

" LOOK AT THE BIRDS
OF THE AIR; THEY DO
NOT SOW OR REAP OR
STORE AWAY IN BARNS,
AND YET YOUR HEAVENLY
FATHER FEEDS THEM.
ARE YOU NOT MUCH
MORE VALUABLE THAN
THEY ?"

"W H O OF Y O U BY
W O R R Y I N G CAN ADD A
S I N G L E H O U R TO
HIS L I F E? AND W H Y DO
YOU WORRY A B O U T
C L O T H E S? SEE HOW THE
L I L I E S OF THE
F I E L D G R O W. THEY
DO NOT L A B O R OR
S P I N."

MATTHEW 6:27-28

371

PG. 281

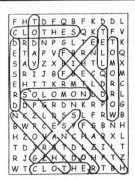

PG. 283

ABCDEFGHIJKLMNOPQRST
UVWXYZ

"SO DO NOT WORRY,
SAYING, 'WHAT
SHALL WE EAT?' OR
'WHAT SHALL WE
DRINK?' OR 'WHAT
SHALL WE WEAR?'"
"DO NOT BE ANXIOUS
ABOUT ANYTHING,
BUT IN EVERY-
THING, BY PRAYER
AND PETITION,
WITH THANKS-
GIVING, PRESENT
YOUR REQUESTS TO
GOD."

PG. 285

"THERE IS NO FEAR IN
LOVE. BUT PERFECT
LOVE DRIVES OUT FEAR,
BECAUSE FEAR HAS TO
DO WITH PUNISHMENT.
THE ONE WHO FEARS IS
NOT MADE PERFECT IN
LOVE."

1 JOHN 4:18

PG. 287

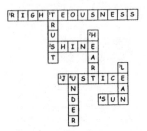

372

"<u>T H O S E</u> WHO <u>K N O W</u>
YOUR <u>N A M E</u> WILL <u>T R U S T</u>
IN YOU, <u>F O R</u> <u>Y O U</u>, LORD,
HAVE <u>N E V E R</u> <u>F O R</u>-
<u>S A K E N</u> THOSE <u>W H O</u>
<u>S E E K</u> <u>Y O U</u>."

PSALM 9:10

"<u>I N</u> <u>Y O U</u> <u>I</u> <u>T R U S T</u>,
<u>O</u> <u>M Y</u> <u>G O D</u>, <u>D O</u> <u>N O T</u>
<u>L E T</u> <u>M E</u> <u>B E</u> <u>P U T</u>
<u>T O</u> <u>S H A M E</u>, <u>N O R</u>
<u>L E T</u> <u>M Y</u> <u>E N E M I E S</u>
<u>T R I U M P H</u> <u>O V E R</u>
<u>M E</u>."

PSALM 25:2

1. <u>C H A R I O T S</u>
   <u>H O R S E S</u>   <u>N A M E</u>

2. <u>T R U S T</u>

3. <u>H E A R T S</u> <u>R E J O I C E</u>
   <u>H O L Y</u>

"<u>DO</u>   <u>NOT</u>   <u>LET</u>   <u>YOUR</u>
<u>HEARTS</u>   <u>BE</u>   <u>TROUBLED</u>.
<u>TRUST</u>   <u>IN</u>   <u>GOD</u>; <u>TRUST</u>
<u>ALSO</u>   <u>IN</u>   <u>ME</u>. <u>IN</u>   <u>MY</u>
<u>FATHER'S</u>   <u>HOUSE</u>   <u>ARE</u>
<u>MANY</u>   <u>ROOMS</u>; <u>IF</u>   <u>IT</u>
<u>WERE</u>   <u>NOT</u>   <u>SO</u>, <u>I</u>
<u>WOULD</u>   <u>HAVE</u>   <u>TOLD</u>
<u>YOU</u>. <u>I</u>   <u>AM</u>   <u>GOING</u>
<u>THERE</u>   <u>TO</u>   <u>PREPARE</u>
<u>A</u>   <u>PLACE</u>   <u>FOR</u>   <u>YOU</u>.
<u>AND</u>   <u>IF</u>   <u>I</u>   <u>GO</u>   <u>AND</u>
<u>PREPARE</u>   <u>A</u>   <u>PLACE</u>
<u>FOR</u>   <u>YOU</u>, <u>I</u>   <u>WILL</u>
<u>COME</u>   <u>BACK</u>   <u>AND</u>   <u>TAKE</u>
<u>YOU</u>   <u>TO</u>   <u>BE</u>   <u>WITH</u>   <u>ME</u>
<u>THAT</u>   <u>YOU</u>   <u>ALSO</u>   <u>MAY</u>
<u>BE</u>   <u>WHERE</u>   <u>I</u>   <u>AM</u>. <u>YOU</u>
<u>KNOW</u>   <u>THE</u>   <u>WAY</u>   <u>TO</u>
<u>THE</u>   <u>PLACE</u>   <u>WHERE</u>   <u>I</u>
<u>AM</u>   <u>GOING</u>."

"_MAY_ THE _GOD_ OF _HOPE_
FILL YOU WITH ALL _JOY_ AND
PEACE AS YOU _TRUST_ IN
HIM, SO THAT YOU MAY
OVERFLOW WITH HOPE BY
THE _POWER_ OF THE _HOLY_
SPIRIT."

ROMANS 15:13

A B C D E F G H I J K L M N O P Q R S T
U V W X Y Z

"_KEEP_ _YOUR_ _LIVES_
FREE _FROM_ _THE_
LOVE _OF_ _MONEY_ _AND_
_BE_ _CONTENT_ _WITH_
WHAT _YOU_ _HAVE_,
BECAUSE _GOD_
HAS _SAID_, '_NEVER_
WILL _I_ _LEAVE_
YOU; _NEVER WILL_
_I_ _FORSAKE_ _YOU_.'"

"_F O R_ THE _L O V E_ OF
16 31 34   25 31 41 15

_M O N E Y_ IS A _R O O T_ OF
26 31 27 15 44   34 31 31 36

ALL _K I N D S_ OF _E V I L_.
24 22 27 14 35   15 41 22 25

SOME _P E O P L E_, _E A G E R_
32 15 31 32 25 15   15 11 17 15 34

FOR _M O N E Y_, HAVE _W A N-_
26 11 27 15 44   47 11 27

_D E R E D_ FROM THE _F A I T H_
14 15 34 15 14   16 11 22 36 21

AND   _P I E R C E D_
32 22 15 34 13 15 14

_T H E M S E L V E S_ WITH
36 21 15 26 35 15 25 41 15 35

_M A N Y_ _G R I E F S_."
26 11 27 44   17 34 22 15 16 35

1 TIMOTHY 6:10

"_T H E N_ HE _S A I D_ _T O_
_T H E M_, '_W A T C H_ _O U T_!
_B E_ _O N_ _Y O U R_ _G U A R D_
_A G A I N S T_   _A L L_
_K I N D S_ _O F_ _G R E E D_;
_A_   _M A N_'S   _L I F E_
_D O E S_   _N O T_   _C O N-_
_S I S T_   _I N_   _T H E_
_A B U N D A N C E_   _O F_
_H I S_   _P O S S E S-_
_S I O N S_.'"

LUKE 12:15

PG. 307

PG. 309

PG. 311

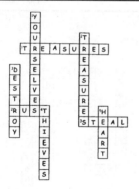

PG. 313

1. P H A R I S E E S
   H Y P O C R I T E S
   C L E A N   D I S H

2. O U T S I D E   I N S I D E
   G R E E D

PG. 315

"TO THE MAN WHO PLEASES HIM, GOD GIVES WISDOM, KNOWLEDGE AND HAPPINESS. BUT TO THE SINNER HE GIVES THE TASK OF GATHERING AND STORING UP WEALTH TO HAND IT OVER TO THE ONE WHO PLEASES GOD. THIS TOO IS MEANINGLESS. A CHASING AFTER THE WIND."

PG. 317

A B C D E F G H I J K L M N O P Q R S T U V W X Y Z

"MOREOVER, WHEN GOD GIVES ANY MAN WEALTH AND POSSESSIONS, AND ENABLES HIM TO ENJOY THEM, TO ACCEPT HIS LOT AND BE HAPPY IN HIS WORK — THIS IS A GIFT OF GOD."

PG. 319

"EACH ONE SHOULD USE WHATEVER GIFT HE HAS RECEIVED TO SERVE OTHERS, FAITHFULLY ADMINISTERING GOD'S GRACE IN ITS VARIOUS FORMS.
1 PETER 4:10

PG. 321

Crossword:

1 Down: DOWNCAST
2 Down: THEREFORE
3 Across: DISTURBED
2 Down/Across: SOUL
4 Across: HOPE
4 Down: HERMON
5 Across: GOD

" SING AND MAKE MUSIC
IN YOUR HEART TO THE
LORD , ALWAYS GIVING
THANKS TO GOD THE
FATHER FOR EVERYTHING ,
IN THE NAME OF OUR LORD
JESUS CHRIST ."

EPHESIANS 5:19-20

"TO YOU, O LORD, I
44 31 37   25 31 34 14
LIFT UP MY SOUL."
25 22 16 36   26 44   35 31 37 25

PSALM 25:1

"TURN TO ME AND BE
36 37 34 27   26 15
GRACIOUS TO
17 34 11 13 22 31 37 35
ME, FOR I AM LONELY
16 31 34   11 26   25 31 27 15 25 44
AND AFFLICTED."
11 16 16 25 22 13 36 15 14

PSALM 25:16

1. PEACE   SAFETY
2. GIVES BLESSES
   PEOPLE
3. GOOD   SEEK
   PURSUE

377

PG. 333

ABCDEFGHIJKLMNOPQRST
UVWXYZ

"T H E R E F O R E,
S I N C E   W E   H A V E
B E E N   J U S T I F I E D
T H R O U G H   F A I T H,
W E   H A V E   P E A C E
W I T H   G O D   T H R O U G H
O U R   L O R D   J E S U S
C H R I S T."

"I F   I T   I S   P O S-
S I B L E,   A S   F A R
A S   I T   D E P E N D S
O N   Y O U,   L I V E   A T
P E A C E   W I T H
E V E R Y O N E."

PG. 335

PG. 337

"LET THE PEACE OF CHRIST
RULE IN YOUR HEARTS, SINCE
AS MEMBERS OF ONE BODY
YOU WERE CALLED TO PEACE."
COLOSSIANS 3:15

"FLEE THE EVIL DESIRES OF
YOUTH, AND PURSUE
RIGHTEOUSNESS, FAITH,
LOVE AND PEACE, ALONG
WITH THOSE WHO CALL ON THE
LORD OUT OF A PURE HEART.
DON'T HAVE ANYTHING TO DO WITH
FOOLISH AND STUPID
ARGUMENTS, BECAUSE YOU
KNOW THEY PRODUCE QUARRELS."
2 TIMOTHY 2:22-23

PG. 339

"PEACE I LEAVE WITH YOU; MY PEACE I GIVE YOU. I DO NOT GIVE TO YOU AS THE WORLD GIVES. DO NOT LET YOUR HEARTS BE TROUBLED AND DO NOT BE AFRAID."

JOHN 14:27

"I HAVE TOLD YOU THESE THINGS, SO THAT IN ME YOU MAY HAVE PEACE. IN THIS WORLD YOU WILL HAVE TROUBLE. BUT TAKE HEART! I HAVE OVER-COME THE WORLD."

JOHN 16:33

"WHEN TEMPTED, NO ONE SHOULD SAY, 'GOD IS TEMPTING ME.' FOR GOD CANNOT BE TEMPTED BY EVIL, NOR DOES HE TEMPT ANYONE; BUT EACH ONE IS TEMPTED WHEN, BY HIS OWN EVIL DESIRE, HE IS DRAGGED AWAY AND ENTICED. THEN, AFTER DESIRE HAS CONCEIVED, IT GIVES BIRTH TO SIN; AND SIN, WHEN IT IS FULL-GROWN, GIVES BIRTH TO DEATH."

JAMES 1:13-15

MULTIPLE CHOICE

"PEOPLE WHO WANT TO GET RICH FALL INTO TEMPTATION AND A TRAP AND INTO MANY FOOLISH AND HARMFUL DESIRES THAT PLUNGE MEN INTO RUIN AND DESTRUCTION."

I TIMOTHY 6:9

AFTER READING THE VERSE ABOVE, WHAT WOULD BE THE RIGHT CHOICES BELOW?

1. YOU GET A LOT OF MONEY FOR YOUR BIRTH DAY.
   A) YOU HIDE IT AWAY, SO YOU DON'T EVER HAVE TO SHARE.
   B) YOU GIVE SOME BACK TO GOD, PUT SOME TOWARDS SAVINGS, AND TAKE A LITTLE TO SPEND.
   C) YOU SPEND IT ALL AT THE LOCAL VIDEO ARCADE.

2. YOUR YOUNGER BROTHER'S BIKE HAS A FLAT TIRE AND HE HAS NO MONEY TO REPAIR IT.
   A) YOU OFFER TO LOAN HIM THE MONEY AND HE CAN PAY IT BACK WHEN HE CAN.
   B) YOU TELL HIM TO TAKE CARE OF HIS OWN PROBLEMS.
   C) YOU GIVE HIM THE MONEY AS LONG AS HE CLEANS YOUR ROOM FOR THE NEXT YEAR.

3. YOU FINALLY GOT THAT NEW GAME SYSTEM!
   A) YOU SHARE IT WITH NO ONE.
   B) YOU SPEND ALL YOUR TIME AT IT... YOUR CHORES AREN'T GETTING DONE AND YOUR GRADES ARE SLIPPING.
   C) YOU CAREFULLY SCHEDULE YOUR TIME ON IT.

4. YOU'VE BEEN ASKED AT CHURCH TO GIVE TO AN EMERGENCY RELIEF FUND.
   A) YOU GIVE TEN PERCENT OF YOUR SAVINGS.
   B) YOU'RE ANGRY BUT GIVE BECAUSE IT IS EXPECTED OF YOU.
   C) YOU ASK GOD WHAT AMOUNT HE WOULD HAVE YOU GIVE.

A B C D E F G H I J K L M N O P Q R S T U V W X Y Z

"BECAUSE HE HIMSELF SUFFERED WHEN HE WAS TEMPTED, HE IS ABLE TO HELP THOSE WHO ARE BEING TEMPTED."

"LET US THEN APPROACH THE THRONE OF GRACE WITH CONFIDENCE, SO THAT WE MAY RECEIVE MERCY AND FIND GRACE TO HELP US IN OUR TIME OF NEED."

" BROTHERS , IF SOMEONE IS CAUGHT IN A SIN , WHO ARE SPIRITUAL SHOULD RESTORE HIM GENTLY . BUT WATCH YOURSELF , OR YOU ALSO MAY BE TEMPTED ."

GALATIANS 6:1

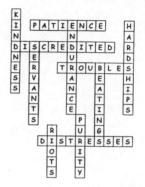

"BEAR IN MIND THAT OUR LORD'S PATIENCE MEANS SALVATION, JUST AS OUR DEAR BROTHER PAUL ALSO WROTE YOU WITH THE WISDOM THAT GOD GAVE HIM."

2 PETER 3:15

If you enjoyed Super Bible
Activities for Kids you might enjoy...

Super Bible Scrambles
and Stories for Kids
ISBN 978-1-60260-396-7

Super Bible Picture Fun for Kids
ISBN 978-1-60260-395-0

Super Bible Trivia for Kids
ISBN 978-1-60260-394-3

Available wherever books are sold.